CW00544538

VERONICA FORREST–THOMSON

SELECTED POEMS

BOOKS BY VERONICA FORREST–THOMSON

POETRY

As Veronica Forrest

Identi–kit
London, Outposts Publications, 1967

Twelve Academic Questions
Cambridge, The Author, 1970

As Veronica Forrest–Thomson

Language–Games
Leeds, New Poets Award 2,
School of English Press, University of Leeds, 1971

Cordelia: or, 'A Poem should not Mean, but Be'
[Leicester], Omens Poetry Pamphlet, no. 2, 1974

On the Periphery
Cambridge, Street Editions, 1976

Collected Poems and Translations
London, Lewes, Berkeley, Allardyce, Barnett, Publishers, 1990

LITERARY CRITICISM

Poetic Artifice: A Theory of Twentieth–Century Poetry
Manchester, Manchester University Press, and
New York, St Martins Press, 1978

VERONICA FORREST–THOMSON

SELECTED POEMS

Language–Games

On the Periphery

and other writings

Edited by Anthony Barnett

Postscript by Alison Mark

Invisible Books

Copyright © 1971

Copyright © Veronica Forrest–Thomson 1974

Copyright © Jonathan Culler 1976

Copyright © Jonathan Culler and The Estate of Veronica Forrest–Thomson 1990, 1999

This edition Copyright © Invisible Books 1999

Editorial matter Copyright © Anthony Barnett 1990, 1999

Postscript Copyright © Alison Mark 1999

This selection published by arrangement with Allardyce, Barnett, Publishers
publishers of Veronica Forrest–Thomson *Collected Poems and Translations*
and The Estate of Veronica Forrest–Thomson

In accordance with the Copyright, Design and Patents Act 1988
The Estate of Veronica Forrest–Thomson
hereby identifies her as the author of this work

Anthology rights, permissions, and other enquiries must be addressed to
The Estate of Veronica Forrest–Thomson
c/o Allardyce, Barnett, Publishers
14 Mount Street | Lewes | East Sussex BN7 1HL | England

photo: Veronica Forrest–Thomson as Postgraduate,
courtesy her family

Published by Invisible Books | B.M. Invisible | London WC1N 3XX | UK
Distributed in the USA by SPD | 1341 Seventh Street | Berkeley CA 94710

Designed by Woodrow Phoenix

A c-i-p record for this book is available from The British Library

Printed by Antony Rowe Ltd | Bumper's Farm | Chippenham | Wiltshire

ISBN 0 9532826 1 9

CONTENTS

EDITOR'S NOTE

This selected volume comprises the whole of two book collections by Veronica Forrest–Thomson: *Language–Games* published in 1971; and *On the Periphery* published, in a compromised edition, posthumously in 1976. Also included are a group of poems from the late 1960s, roughly contemporary with the writing in *Language–Games*; and "Further Poems", some, though certainly not all, of which might well have been intended as additions to *On the Periphery*. The opportunity has also been taken to include an appendix of a few early poems in fugitive journals located since the publication in 1990 of *Collected Poems and Translations*; as well as an appendix of corrections to poems in that volume not reprinted in the present selection. Corrections to the poems that are reprinted here have been made silently. Inconsistencies that could be the author's intention have been kept.

Poems not reprinted in the present volume are her first pamphlet *Identi–kit*, published in 1967; a large group of early poems garnered from periodicals and manuscripts; and translations from French poets. All that work will be found in *Collected Poems and Translations*. That volume also incorporates an editorial apparatus, which is the result of exhaustive research, including significant variants of some poems; and a bibliography of her critical writings. The "Notes" in the *Collected* explain the guiding principles behind the establishment of what is now likely to remain the authoritative text.

I am grateful to Neil J. Crawford, Paul Holman, John London, J.H. Prynne, Peter Riley, and Clive Watkins for communicating their findings since the publication of *Collected Poems and Translations*, in respect of corrections or poems. A few issues of fugitive journals are still unlocated, and the possibility that there exist further early poems cannot be ruled out.

Anthony Barnett

UNCOLLECTED POEMS

Sprinkle a pinch of dust, or three,
on Archytas F.R.S.
who specialised in nebulae;
memorial—an out-of-date laboratory.
Tantalus studies divinity
transubstantiating our family flesh;
prefers the gods out of reach.
Lord Chief Justice Minos
was not given leave to appeal.
Pythagoras believed in reincarnation
hence lost only bones nerves blood brain.
The rest of him's still waiting.

As you pass their floating corpses, astronaut,
erase especially unnecessary words;
"But wholly one the night remains,
death's road to be walked once for all".
How unremarkable that
"Furies serve some as a spectacle for Mars"
or "The greedy sea is a destruction to sailors",
phrases whose only use is in a grammar.
Predicatively dative
we define function not being.
Death is not immortalised by apostrophe
or life by ideas.
We know our place, Horatius,
better even than you;
find nothing incongruous in
"Minds about to die
measuring the innumerable sands of stars",
claim no immunity
from dust storms meteorites magnetic shift,
because we have them all worked out.
Facts do not need emotion.
Thus: please don't clutter up the sky
with littered personality.
I know you're in a hurry, but anyway
you don't have long;
so pulverise the past dear
before you hurry on.

"July: I would have painted
in a yellow jacket eating cherries."
je m'en fiche de toutes ces affiches, icons
of worship on Boul' Mich. As the incense
of Gauloises burns these saints
of the new dispensation are haloed
in self-approbation although
THE PRESENT KING OF FRANCE IS BALD
Sur le plan du Métro it is clear
just where we want to go,
that one may claim reassurance
from a multicoloured name, objective
design from an abstract line although
one may écrire n'importe où
sont les noms de yester-year?
(les noms d'antan sont n'importe où)
Bien que on songe
à cette mélange des langues and hear
a quotation for every occasion, cliché
or paradox, with a coin in the intellectual jukebox
(if one can find a bureau de change)
si l'on a de la chance de trouver
la station de correspondance
for the verbal dance, de raccrocher
"In a station of the Metro"
ce passant, the apparition
of the literary tradition, still
THE PRESENT KING OF FRANCE IS BALD
et le quatorze juillet
on paie what is due to our nostalgie
de la boue avec les mots
qui coûtent trop. Phrases
come too dear for where
are the words of yester-year?
The rate of exchange between thing
and sign devalues a currency
of mental outline so then there is love
dancing wine et tous les restes

du second-best, et, as one can,
l'on se sauve parce que
LE ROI PRESENT DE LA FRANCE EST CHAUVE

(Opening quotation from Dr. Johnson's Dictionary;
refrain from philosophical discussions on "referring",
on the connection between thing and sign.)

Thus party with witte
party with nygraumancy
King's College is on fire;
I have an image of dining in Hall with Dr. Dee.
We shall talk at a later occasion
of the way in which words and things may be connected.
Tonight we should like to say,
What the picture tells us is itself,
This language-game is played
instead of, We have this experience.

It patterns facts, names, architecture, dates
(As in the lawcourts in Paris
a motor accident is represented
by means of dolls.)
A context in which we occur
—"the slightly hysterical style of University talk"—
teaches us our meaning;
a fourth dimension for the blue
of that bound typescript.

The gap between red and green
is then grammatical;
white objects through coloured spectacles.
But though our syntax stains the window-glass,
those stones across the court
assert their tenses
party per fess argent and vert,
party per chevron or and gueules.

In order to be clear about aesthetic words
you have to describe ways of living.
said Wittgenstein
              who was "indifferent to his surroundings".
remembering the date (1969) on the calendar
an attempt to condense the James novel
(a young American T.S. Eliot,
write him at Merton, Oxford.
I think him worth watching
              and
his *Portrait of a Lady* is very nicely drawn.)
in the literary scene of Allen Ginsberg
(Apocalyptic tradition of Whitman, of course)
could only be tried here
(If you people at Cam can do
                anything
in the way of a milieu.)
The need of old forms, old situations,
as Yeats wrote (1929)
           also,
Ezra when he recreates Propertius
escapes from his scepticism.
Whether "historical or philosophical" in approach
this is still
some form of exercise that don't depend
on the state of your liver;
the bus late an idea in labour
and no pencil or paper
(but to dial 999 for an ambulance that night
was much more exciting.)

I don't believe in personal relationships,
said the young anthropologist
              (female),
I believe in fantasy.
But to fall in love with one's teachers
that also is a matter of economy.

There are not enough nouns around which to create images.
For verbs express activity and the act
is unambiguous. Experience is an active
verb. Mummy and Coffin of an Un-named
Priestess (*c.*1050 B.C.). There are not
enough pronouns to create images around.
Only the ivory handle of a bronze mirror,
said the Lady
of Shalott.
Now we move on to the Cycladic Antiquities.
Marble figure of a woman from Cambridge
(*c.*1969 A.D.). "Such a comparison *might*
help to show that common fundamental
sculptural ideas persist." (Antiparos 2500-
2000 B.C.) (Henry Moore 1969 A.D.).
The simplicity of wedge on ovoid, nose
in face and the functionality of buttocks
is belied by a shifting poise and glitter
an instability of marble. I am, however, sick
of mirrors. And metaphor is a *low* relief.
Manuscript Room, Bassae Room, Tea &
Coffee Room.
        But all I mean
        is that no-one
        wants to be deceived
        in his own mind.
(Plato, *Republic* II *c.*380 B.C.). Monochrome
is a desired medium though they coloured
their statues and we colour our
dreams
        In things which touch
        most nearly the most
        important part of him
        no man really wants
        to be deceived but
        is terrified of it.

But there *aren't* enough names. So what
is left except fiction, verbal activity
being too crude for us. The act
is ambiguous (vide supra). To leave
a clay jar inscribed "Megakles
is handsome" and signed by "Phistias
as potter" since
                    we have already
                    forbidden madness
                    and the representation
                    of madness,
is the alternative to mummification. It
is the poised instability of marble. So,
of the second case "in which the poet speaks
in his own person", "the best example
is lyric poetry." Although "A man cannot
play many characters as well as he can, one",
this statue of an un-named *person* (There are
not enough pronouns.) is carved in imitation
of Cycladic Art and in compassion
for Egyptian Metonymies.

INDIVIDUALS

are complex
        not as a tangle of wire
but as a coiled spring
        before it is stretched out
into simplicity.
        Strawson's cat slices
slip through your fingers
        with a prickle of fur;
basic particulars:
        persons
and material bodies.
        Pound's cats at Rapallo
too hungry to bother
        with their place in a conceptual scheme
appear nevertheless
        in the Cantos
"some of them are so ungrateful"
said T.S. Eliot.

        Practical Cats
can omit
        "the exasperating clause":
"if all objectivity and all knowledge is relative . . ."
        Mr. Eliot
never returned to take his doctor's degree.
("Forty six years after my academic philosophizing
  came to an end, I find myself unable to think
  in the terminology of this essay. Indeed
  I do not claim to understand it.")
He
  slips through your fingers
        with a prickle of fur.
  But there is at least a case
        that poetry should trace
  the double helix
  (those interlocking strands of DNA)
        before it try
  to straighten the spring.

LANGUAGE–GAMES

daisy:
      garden aster of a shrubby habit
October:
       bearing masses of small purplish flowers
blackbird:
        the ring ouzel
crocus:
      the autumn crocus
moon:
    the
    harvest
    moon

Michaelse maesse her on lande wunode
se eorl syththan oth thet ofer sce
in 1123
      masses of small purplish flowers
      the ring ouzel
      the autumn crocus
      the
      harvest
      moon

tide:
    time
spring:
      Indian Summer
term:
      a term or session of the High Court of Justice
      in England and also of Oxford,
      Cambridge

the kinges power and is ost wende vorth
to Oxenforde aboute mielmasse
in 1297
       time
       Indian summer
       also of Oxford, Cambridge
       at the gret cowrtes at Mykelmas the year
       in 1453
              Trinity
              Nevile's
              Queens'
                    and
bearing masses of small purplish flowers
the harvest
moon.

(All quotations from the OED.*)*

But in a fairy tale the pot too can hear and see[1]
and help the hero on his way[2]
to stimulate something to thoughts of his own,
Noms de Personnes, Noms de Pays

as Proust taught le tout Paris
his little phrase
trying to get between pain and its expression.[3]
Life lies between Combray and Illiers.[4]

It is not impossible reflections in a madeleine
bring light into one brain[5, 6]
but a man who wants discrete particulars[7]
cries out in pain

with the aphasiac surface of a day's
objects and events,
can only choose the mouth which says:[8]
I should have liked to produce a good book.

This has not come about
but the time is past in which I could improve it.

[1] Certainly but it can also talk

[2] But of course it is not likely

[3] We are not concerned with the difference, internal/external

[4] Language-game no. 30

[5] Or another

[6] In its poverty and in the darkness of lost time

[7] When the light strikes Fizeau's mirror

[8] A stamp which marks them mine.

(Quotations freely adapted from Brown Book, Investigations, and Proust.)

DUCKS & RABBITS

in the stream;[1]
look, the duck-rabbits swim between.
The Mill Race
at Granta Place
tosses them from form to form,
dissolving bodies in the spume.

Given A and see[2]
find be[3]
(look at you, don't look at me)[4]
Given B, see A and C.
that's what metaphor[5]
is for.

Date and place
in the expression of a face[6]
provide the frame
for an instinct to rename,[7]
to try to hold apart
Gestalt and Art.

---

[1] Of consciousness

[2] The expression of a change of aspect is the expression of a new perception.

[3] And at the same time of the perception's being unchanged.

[4] Do not ask yourself "How does it work with me?" Ask "What do I know about someone else?"

[5] Here it is useful to introduce the idea of a picture-object.

[6] A child can talk to picture-men or picture-animals. It can treat them as it treats dolls.

[7] Hence the flashing of an aspect on us seems half visual experience, half thought.

Sure
if we are to speak of the experience of thinking
the experience of speaking is as good as any,
thus:
"Who is Wittgenstein?"
                 (she said, having been present
                 at some months' acrimonious
                 debate on *Philosophical Investigations*)
With the configuration of chess-pieces
limbs describe themselves in rooms
under the angle-poise.
"What is the opposite of brown?
—orange?
—another shade
of brown."
Limbs of the angle alter,
poise, in rooms:
what is the opposite of me?
—you?
—another shade
of me.
Suppose it were
part of my day-dream to say
"I am merely engaged in fantasy."
I can write
"I am healthy."
in the dialogue of a play
and so not mean it,
although it is true.
This is dialogue in a play
—the language-game
with pronouns.
A spot-light swivels
through faces of the cast and rests in
the mirror.

One can own a mirror
does one then own the reflections
that may be seen in it?
I love you.
—the language-game
with pronouns and
"Confucius he say":
The concept of a living being
has the same indeterminacy
as that of a language.
Love is not a feeling.
Love is put to the test
—the *grammatical* test.

Anyone who does not understand
why we talk about these things
must feel what we say to be mere trifling,
thus:
"It seems a bit of a fuss about nothing."

                                   (she said after reading
                                   The Language of Criticism)

Roomspace in which we dispose
ourselves is not external.
The gap between
my purple trousers
and his pale-green shirt
is then
grammatical.
I love you.
One says the ordinary thing
—with the wrong gesture.
Folded & re
folded the
map of the
town is pass
ed through
our lives

& hands ac
ross the table.

The *same* indeterminacy though,
which could suggest a cast-
list drawn up in language
play, that speech commits
to fantasy. And so it does
at least in the first
person singular, for:
One's hand writes
it does not write because one wills
but one wills
what it writes.

(Quotations from Wittgenstein, Zettel.)

ACROSTIC

And can the first attitude of all
be directed towards a possible disillusion
so that one learns from the beginning,
"That is probably a chair."
Thys crede is called Simbolum
that is to say a gatherynge of morselles.
Choice of words is the best paradigm
for other choices. What other choices?
I have as many friends as the number
yielded by the solution of this
equation. For the college system
makes "pretty inchoate" a topic—
itself—of the present dissertation.

And now how does one learn the question?
"Is it really also a chair?" Well
bit by bit daily life becomes such
that there is a place for hope in it.
The name begins to mean its bearer.
(A connection between the concept
of meaning and the concept of teaching.)
Is someone speaking untruth?
If I say "I am not conscious."
"I am not in love any more."
And suppose a parrot says:
"I don't understand a word."
or a gramophone: "I am only
a machine." I am only
a machine and paint my love
by numbers, a gathering of morsels.
For the meaning of a name
is not its bearer. (And truth
if I say it while unconscious)
I like things this way.
They are probably, chairs?

(*Quotations from* Zettel.)

"Wittgenstein would say"
$\qquad$(L.W. 1889-1951)
but he is dead;
therefore and nevertheless
can be said in literary monograph to say
anything.
No more helpless in this respect
than we, the stakes in our own
language-games—Eng. Lit. in this case
but History or Science
will serve the purpose equally well.
"Perfection of the life or of the work."
$\qquad$(W.B.Y. 1865-1939)
"Perfection is possible in neither."
$\qquad$(W.H.A. 1907-   )
These are some of the
Lessons of the Masters
$\qquad$(and another is that sexuality
$\qquad$is a branch of aesthetics;
$\qquad$but that really is a digression.)
Further both meanings
of hieros
$\qquad$(Gk. sacred, accursed)
apply to the Sacred Fount, "from
whence my being flows
or else dries up."
$\qquad$(H.J. 1843-1916
$\qquad$W.S. 1564-1616)
Minny Temple dies for him.
He found it necessary for red hair
to become pigment on a canvas
by Bronzino. It is necessary
for us to become pigment
and when confronted, on any
social occasion, with the canvas

(in the art of the novel
there is no scene
that is not plot,
no dialogue
that is not scene.)

to say, as of Wittgenstein,
"and dead, dead, dead."
But "art is disposable nowadays"
which makes the definition that much
more difficult; especially as a
psychiatric hospital sifts more
efficiently "the mad abstract dark."

(or else dries up)

ANTIPHRASIS

I went to the British Museum
I looked at the Egyptian Antiquities;
neat syntax of ibis and scarab
sum up my several identities;
the stone face is dumb,
the mummy enclosed in its chattering sarcophagus.
I stared at the Rosetta Stone
I was irritated by a crowd of French schoolchildren
My feet hurt.
I am working at the collation
of these parallel texts
"the t'one in ye proper simple speech
and t'other by the fygure of irony"

(Thos. More, 1533)

Socratic method
(This is to be the theme.)
"esp. in reference to the dissimulation of ignorance
practised by Socrates

(c.400 B.C.)

as a means of confounding an adversary."

(OED)

Thought is a subversion of reality
and "time is the evil, beloved"

(E.P.)

Shall I compare you to Apollo (or Perithoös)
on the west pediment of The Temple of Zeus?
I dreamt you were made of stone
and struck your head off with a pen.
It rolled and lay still and bled
sawdust. There is a sawdust pit
below the sculptures to protect
them from earthquakes which are
frequent in the area. The attribution
of identity (Apollo or Perithoös)
to "you" is disputed.
("Other Minds" etc. vide supra)
Each figurative speech forms
"a contradictory outcome of events

as if in mockery of the promise and fitness of things."

(OED)

I went to the British Museum
I fled from words to stone
I read the chatter of ibis and scarab
on the Egyptian tombs.
"By the fygure *Ironia* which we call the *drye Mock*"

(Puttenham, Arte of English Poesie, 1589)

ANTIQUITIES

A gesture is adjective,
two hands, granite
when they turn bread to flesh
(Notre Dame, July 14th)
A mirror is a museum-case,
two hands, priestesses'
when she mummifies her face.
Emotion is a parenthesis,
two hands, irony
when I light the candle
and cross myself.
Aesthetic approbation is glass
when it encloses her faience eyes
and gilded skin.
(Musée du Louvre, July 18th)
Glance is the copula
that petrifies our several identities,
syntactic superficies.

       II

Michaelmas
My cardboard daisies are in bloom
again.
The city's silhouette stands out
just like real, from a child's
pop-up book, "a castle cut in
paper" (*Gawain & the Grene Knight*
c.1400). Autumn leaves turn like
pages, black on white. For green
and gold must be as parenthetical
as walks through sharpening air
and clamant colour, smoky light
along the Backs, from typewriter
to Library. "Grammar" derives from
"glamour"; ecology may show the two

still cognate: Museum, Gk. mouseion,
a seat of the Muses, a building
dedicated to the pursuit of learning
or the arts. (OED)
The glamorous grammatical frames
captions for a monograph on non-
existent plates. Glue, paper,
scissors, and the library together
paste a mock-up of an individual
history. The art of English Poesie?
"Such synne is called yronye."

Certainly
      it is the "cultural level
of a Noah's Ark"
(The animals go in two by two.)
But
   we do inhabit a rainy climate.
And alas
      you can't get a sex change
on the N.H.S.
        Only verbal instruments (Elizabeth Eberhardt
        referred to throughout her diary as "he")
        or linguistic situation (comprising clothes,
        attitudes, behaviour) can perform the delicate
        operation, of altering the terms in an erotic
        equation.
We
   were fitting key
words to our lives
e.g.
Tension, awareness, extremity
(liberté, égalité, fraternité)
She
   hesitated for a long while
then put down her cards;
Michael   amo
     Hamid   amas
        Me   amat

"Of course I know what it means.
I did A level Latin."

Catch phrase
         love all
                   game and set.
There are no
       just(es)
                mots.

THE HYPHEN

For the centenary of Girton College

i hyphen (Gk. together, in one)
a short dash or line used to connect
two words together as a compound
1869-
1969
to connect Chapel Wing and Library.
But also: to divide
for etymological or other purpose.
A gap in stone makes actual
the paradox of a centenary.
"It was a hyphen connecting different races."
and to the library
"a bridge for migrations".
In search of an etymology
                          for compound lives,
this architecture,
                     an exercise in paleography
(Victorian Gothic)
                     asserts the same intention.
Portraits busts and books
                          the "context in which we occur"
that teaches us our meaning,
                          ignore the lacunae
of a century
               in their state-
ment of our need to hyphenate.

ALKA-SELTZER POEM

With beaded bubbles winking at the brim
the effervescence is subsiding. Drink
before effervescence subsides. Inert
liquid and undissolved tablets are dangerous.
It is like the unperceived rearrangement
of ice, a gradual crackle spreading under
our feet, signalising thaw. In cold weather
Andrew's Liver Salts may be taken in water
with the chill off. Freeze alternatively
or crystallize the alteration in acidic
percentages which is this process of
dissolving. The cause is physiology,
and the effect, metaphor. Alleviation
of the effects of over-indulgence
in alcohol or words is one of her
cloudy trophies. Silver tinsel hangs
like nets of frost, like votive
offerings for our escape from water
in all the shop-windows. "You can use,"
she said, "glue to stick it on with—
Durex." This metaphor requires completion
in a chemists' with a request for a packet
of Durofix (gossamer). For experience
is an active verb and the end
of poetry is activity. Hung-over
this morning in a gossamer net
of words, the bubbles wink & subside.

and witte familiar letters
lately passed between two
Universitie men: touching
the Earthquake in April last
and our English reformed
Versifying. (1) Long lackt alas
hath been thy faithful aide in hard essay
Whiles deadly fit thy pupil doth dismay.
I like your late pentameters so exceeding
well that I also enure my Penne sometime
in that kind:
A cuts off
B's arm, shaves
it & sends
it to C,
C being the
logical con
stant, the
situation we
are to infer
from terms
in metaphoric
relation.
We are, for
instance, two
on a raft &
starving, A
a surgeon
with hairless
arms and
ingenuity. Being thus so closely and eagerly
set at our game we scarcely need perceive
the rest: Spanish Burgundy, Georges Brassens,
tripos finished, a lack of love and cigarettes.
P, however, implies Q. The entailment
relation between fact and fiction is perhaps
called metaphor, (B is hirsute and hard-
up.) or some new kind of Cambridge

Platonism:
P cuts off
Q's arm
and puts
it in a
film (a
stocking
stuffed with
handkerchiefs)
sent to X
to the im
mortal mem
ory of Ed
mund Spen
ser (C's
concept of
moral respons
ibility is
exigent.) And V had better mind her p's
and q's. For the entailment works one way
only, poetic licence being allverywellbut.
Sith none that breatheth *living* air
does know where is that happy land of Faëry.
(2) We are all ribosomes
of the same phoneme.
(3) I think the earthquake was also
there with you, overthrowing divers
old buildings and peeces of Churches.
Architecture is the jumping-off point,
for example, The Senate House Leap, to
Caius; it is responsible for a lot. How
oft do they their silver bowers leave
To come to succour us that succour want.
We must admit that the self is not
enclosed by a wall, although castles
of extendible polystyrene may be respons
ible for a lot. A castle is called
Alma. Its

walls are
painted
faire with
memorable
gestes, of
artes, of
science, of
Philosophy
and all that
in the world
was aye thought wittily. *That* hight
Phantastes by its nature true. For when
our minds go wandering uncontrolled, when
we pursue imaginary histories or exercise
our thoughts on some mere supposed
sequence, we give rise to a problem.
Heaven being used shorte as one
sillable when it is in verse.

very commendable letters of the same
mens writing: both touching the fore
said Artificial Versifying and certain
other particulars. Enclosed find
my writing up of the W.P.'s M.Phil.
Many thanks for your informed,
intelligent and convivial contribution
to the discussions: The Examination,
to be conducted at 12, Benet Place,
will take the form of an *essay* on
life (No previous knowledge of the
subject will be assumed.) It should
show, within the clear limitations
of the topic, equivalent qualities
of scholarly competence, critical
intelligence and independence of,
thought as required for the Ph.D.
A "high" standard will be maintained.
(It was a convivial contribution.
Whether it nectar or divine tobacco
were, from whence descend all hopeless
remedies.) And yet me thinkes all
should be Gospell that commeth from
you Doctors of Cambridge. Heaven
being used shorte when it is . . .
(Yet verses are not vaine.)
A breaks
down B's
castle &
c rebuilds
it in Ari
zona.
"Architecture
being less
dispensable
than people."
(2) Reason! quoth Madame Incredula.

This is Cambridge
This is Cambridge
The train now standing at Platform 4 terminates
here
Will all passengers change
please.

NN. is a *full-time* student
(We are always expecting him to come
to tea; we look at our watches; we
wonder if he smokes.) And Upon
Westminster Bridge, when the light falls
across the green field, he regards the swing
and stillness of the axes of time and place
as lines drawn on the lens of a telescope.
He wonders if this ecstacy is worth
cultivating and "how many" have killed
themselves from "pure joy" (If one is used
to a small river, the Thames is always something
of a shock.) The focus tightens and . . .
rests on the tedium of its metaphor.
It's a mugs game, this stance, after—
Mauberley? NN. is not a mug. This is
to certify that he *is* a full time student.

Will all passengers change
please?
The focus sharpens and the turning axes
are lying still. Will all passengers terminate
Here?

(We pause a moment; we think; we lay out)
cigarettes.

And for my sixteenth point,
                    Scharazade:
there was a time when
I did *not* want to grow up
because I should have to stop
telling myself stories. But
(were "but" of the stuff)
typing-ribbon at midnight
burns as beautifully as any
Arabian taper.
            Here we can consult the admirable
            article de *vulgarisation* de Eccles
            on the structure of the cerebral cortex.
Yes, I too am slightly tired
of wind-screen wipers. When,
as noted above, the location
of choice implied a technique
for book-binding the universe.
                    I am indebted for this point
                    to my friend, Dante Alighieri.
Now, I get tired of wind-screen
wipers; hence the sun (also) rises.
                    While this was in proof
                    the admirable article appeared.
Furthermore, if you can't say it
                    You can't say it.

and you can't
whistle it
either

"Keep this letter. It is important"

to Humpty Dumpty, who said
that we could only learn to get the better
of *words,* for the thing which.

And is the oyster also the pearl,
then what about the oyster
                              catcher

(The walrus and the carpenter were sitting in a pub.
Said the walrus to the carpenter: Aye there's the rub.
If I'd had your opportunities you wouldn't now catch me
Gulping down the oysters and swilling the Chablis.
Deep I should go diving in an image of the sea.)

How high they flow here, butter
and tears that is, everything, that is,
2.3*d* for a packet of
                              crumpets, the

(Said carpenter to walrus: I speak, of course, professionally
And I charge for my aqua-lung a nominal fee.
The gap between oyster and pearl as you know,
Is a matter for Linguistics. Skål, Malvolio!
We're not sick yet of self-love, or even L.W.)

world. If the catcher opened the oyster
would he "deeply sympathise", would he see
it was thinking of what
                              pearl

(Nothing but: Cut us another slice.)

Words are a monstrous excrescence.
Everything green is extended. It
is apricot, orange, lemon, olive and cherry,
and other snakes in the linguistic grass;
also a white touch of marble which evokes
no ghosts, the taste of squid, the . . .
Go away. I shall call a policeman.
Acrocorinth which evokes no
goats under the lemon blossom.

World is a monstrous excrescence;
he is following me everywhere, one
Nescafé and twenty Athenes, everything
green; I am not responsible for it.
I don't want to speak to you.
Leave me alone. I shall stay here.
I refuse a green extension. Beware.
I have paid you. I have paid you
enough, sea, sun, and octopodi.
It is raining cats and allomorphs.

"Where" is the British Embassy.

their fractured grace: the wind
disintegrates raindrops: the raindrops
dissolve, a metal grid, that falls.

If all meaning is diacritical, one
will see dualism in anything intelligible.

The eye is like Aprile, that falleth, a priori,
on the flower, the grass, the bird, the
fire-escape—its frame shifted by drops

that glance, with their bright eye-balls
fractured in the wind: the blank world
which its whiteness defends.

All dualisms are not equivalent
nor do they imply one another.

Whiteness defends the grass, the bird, the
raindrops, a light that falls refracts
our fractured grace: our glance: the wind.

his is an uncommon name, uncited in linguistic
examples. It is not he
                who kissed the girl who lives in college
                was surprised to find himself supervised by George
                could not have thought that Newton *is* considered
                the greatest English physicist, exhibited
                a tough reasonableness beneath his slight lyric grace.
He is going into the F.O. and will not be required
for linguistic examples. Reading about Politics
will not help him to pass the Moral, Science, Tripos.
He wouldn't put it this way; in fact he did
put it this way: "I thought Newton is considered
the greatest English beach-comber."

                        "Yes I saw two
ducks the other day." "My 'o's have changed this year."
"Il était d'un air terrible, affreusement consterné."
"Are party conversations like this in Politics?"
The pebbles slide through our fingers, worry
beads brought back from Greece as souvenir and
conversation peace; and we are surprised sometimes
to find that we could not have kissed the girl who
lives in college, that Politics *is* a great ocean
of undiscovered linguistic examples, that we
are Mantrippe's supervisor.

                  I lay in bed, fishing
with the Alka-Seltzer glass beside me. Brother
Urusov came and we talked about the vanity
of the world; there was nothing to say after,
he had pointed out Battersea Power Station.
People who were here before Wittgenstein came
still have command of their "Faculties".
There are no unacceptable sentences, only
impossible worlds; Einstein *has* visited
Troy; we *have* filled our mouths with worry, beads
and it doesn't
                matter
                    about
                        Mantrippe.

ON THE PERIPHERY

the:
the mentioning—run
ubiquitous, Victorian, similar
chism.
Shall topoi, conventional
—momentarily—
elaboration?

Had they conceits?

IN DEFENCE OF GRAHAM HOUGH: STYLE AND STYLISTICS

Study Linguistics
                    to texture received: reader
                                          unity
                                          literary

Literary General
                    to impression: strivings, as—
                                    the language
                                    kind
                                    technical
                                    imagery

Different is a close: the
"of we literary"

cannot of
        —of time subjective—
against the
        —the that

      limited?

NOTE

These three pieces are aleatory poems. They were constructed by noting the last word on the top left-hand corner of consecutive pages in, respectively, *The Common Pursuit* by F.R. Leavis, *Style and Stylistics* by Graham Hough, and Kant's *Critique of Judgement*. The words thus obtained were then arranged as juxtapositions of contexts from which, by following certain conventions of poetic reading, meaning could be obtained. The justification of this enterprise is the fuller knowledge thereby gained of all our processes of understanding—especially—very contemporary poetic techniques. And for this reason they are placed at the beginning of this book.

TO R.Z. AND M.W.

the figure of
                our two friends in
the darkness of
                our familiar city
walking with
                their arms around
each other
                "perhaps"

how is *this*
                relationship "going":
between
                two friends &
the figure:
                the familiar city of
each other
                walking.

ON NAMING OF SHADOWS

Thus the morning's shadow of
        a pigeon's wing
became pretext for each darkness
        in the day,
for the naming of wings &
        moths and move-
ment of leaves, justified each
        by its shade.

I have actually just two
        elements, platinum &
chromium, also some uninterpreted
        spectra, a box
of them, lying around, more
        than I can
fit into a formulated crystal
        the colour of

leaves (green) pigeons (multi) moths
        etc. It is
a jump of several orders of magni-
        tude from shade
to this: a ray of light
        entering a
tourmaline, split up in
        two ways

one, the ordinary, perpendicular
        the other,
extraordinary, parallel, vibrates
        to the prin-
cipal axis of a bifurcated
        obsession.
Its general appearance (the stone)
        colourless &

clear, or black & opaque; but
    (the jump)
also various shades of brown
    red, yellow
green, blue, banded hues where
    we deal
not with absorption, but emission, for there
    is visible, light.

Tenacity was sticking to the topic
                                of blankets
and walnuts, French: noix
                                noisette: a hazel nut.
One word can include two unities;
                                the difficulty
is to recognise when this is the case:
                                a little nut; or take
blankets: the weave of two senses
                                under them
makes nothing of six-term dinner
                                table textures
but do they, even securely tucked
                                at the corners,
comprehend a unity?

                Sweat is not more impure
than tears;
                and indeed it is often followed by them.
The words
                were too hot for blankets
or unity.
                An acorn developed into every oak.

FOR THE SPIDER WHO FREQUENTS OUR BATH

First there is secure, scuttling
                              in the rustic darkness (
the waste-pipe, no
                Freudian repository)
which lacks only a corner
                        to hang a web on.

But the end is enamelled
                        allegory; its dazzle (
a white field for
                Chaucerian spring)
which coloured globes of
                        Bubble-Bath do not evade.

We like watching the sea going away from us
and also retreating certain promises the sky held:
of breaking waves.
Now, this is the regular "Norman landscape";
mist rises through straight-planted trees.
We like watching the road going away from us
in ripples yellow like "specks of foam"
and also retreating certain by-roads from this fracture
of events.
We construct an event out of, behind these shutters "people"
are sleeping.
from an intersection between "the most perfect château of the transition period
and "a cricket on a ball of dung". Our capacity
for indifference is truly astounding

> Until the rock
> will turn to
> air at a ruin-
> ed tower
> & we step
> over its sill
> the doors &
> sills of light.

So would you mind just standing in the café doorway
for a minute longer against the sun because I'm
writing a poem about intersections (the doors & sills of light)
between the mind and stone, imagination and reality; and because
everything's fine for my palms drip sweat and all the leg muscles
tremble so nicely in the unconstructed event of such a journey.

We do not watch with complacency the sea retreating, leaving
the stonework stranded in its imaginary light like
your shadow in the café door. So again laughter muscles
go through their contractions nicely, for it's all right;
you can move now. Such savage triumph returns us to Maillezais.
The abbey stands still, without quotation marks.

Printed in natural colours, we find a way always
to deny the world; even its "aerial view" from
"the tower itself". A biro-cross marks the place
where our arcades and buttresses dissolved in air;
but still it is a "carte-postale de luxe" bought as
reminder of an "extraordinary experience".
These occasions have a way of multiplying.
The treads uneven, between steps with "five-hundred years of wear";
and darkened to an height of—wouldn't you say—
about the same number of feet. This would never be allowed
in England: such sudden and insouciant lack
of the next step. Give me your hand.

Shall we exorcise the colours that contrast us
with the evening walk? Any next walk must be this one,
now that we have given it the article, consciously
evoked in word and gesture: our shadowy design to
undermine the objects on our path.
So that this dead leaf, in lack of colour and
perfected shape is like fan-vaulting discerned
in the abbey—communication having been accepted—
But no finality in such a text can justify
a reference to Clément and his castle, Villandraut.

PFARR-SCHMERTZ (VILLAGE-ANGUISH)

Making love & omelettes

> For every poem ought to contain
> at least one zeugma

we may discern a very
palpable corner of a
sheet. Like love it

> It ought to; and since "is"
> may be derived from "ought",
> the sheet, the situation and
> ourselves exist (see, *Proc. Arist. Soc.*,
> supp. vol. XCCCI)

is like the palpable
light set square
in wooden tapestry

> stained glass (see La Sainte Chapelle)

like irony discerned
in fan-vaulting.
Interlocking rings
of glazed perception
turn in our eyes &
fingers, to be unravelled, Chinese

> It was, therefore, quite right
> of Chiang Hen to write down
> the text only. For if the student
> concentrates and uses his mind
> he will discover the process
> between the lines (see, *The
> Unwobbling Pivot*, trans. E.P.)

puzzles. Have you
seen the minnows
in the steel-dust,
the rose, the magnet
leaves, in the mere?

> Irony as an acceptance of limitation
> is our natural approach to the divine
> (see, Elizabeth David, *French Provincial
> Cooking*)

If we are going
to get up we ought
to get up, and
                              Thus we are derived from "ought"
eat our glazed
perceptions in
the form of
croissants, leaving
the palpable corner
to the sheet.

To seek mysteries in the obscure, poking into magic and committing
eccentricities in order to be talked about later—This I do not.

THE DYING GLADIATOR

Di pensier in pensier
from impasse to impasse, from Christmas tree
to jelly-fish, stranded on the sandy bed
of the semiotic sea, his network in the dust;
his vehicle for macroscopic structures,
dismembered by bicycle handlebars
as we crossed King's Parade

                    Did someone speak to me?

From valley to valley;
his eyes upon his native hills, every
marked path hostile to the tranquil life

                    Of reassurance in physical properties
                    like chrysanthemums in a yellow jug

where mist folds knot in nodes
of light, in the multivalence
of an implicated calculus
but *torn* out of our hands
by his entangled fish-spear

                    Like the date on the calendar or
                    a chair for someone I love to sit
                    reading, or a new salad-bowl

from mouth to ashtray
from thread to needle,
from

                    A point of light that reaches through
                    water to the sea-bed where
                    like carnivorous anemones
                    we open

leaning on an elbow,
he dies   and close.

Le vin est objectivement bon   mais la bonté du vin
est un mythe. The veins are obviously bloodless
but the blood in the veins   is mine. A vision
of ordinary beauty resembles the v in the mind.
The v is obvious in but.   It makes beauty
in verbs a myth. Vacillations of opening blood
burst the beauty of v   that is mine. V
in an ordinary bottle   is the breakdown of verbs
in the mind. Violent   and opening beauty, the bursting
of verbs is a myth. Violence objective and but
is this beauty of   veins in the mind.

"If you smash that glass, my dear, you know
you'll simply have to sweep it up again afterwards.
And anyway it's a waste of good wine!"

If it were quicksand you could sink;
something needing a light touch
soon and so simply takes its revenge.
Slightly west of Goodwin Sands
the land hardens again with history,
resists the symbol.
Chalk requires an allegorical hand,
or employee of Sussex Water Board
who sets a notice here:
DANGER SUBMERGED STRUCTURES
and all at once Transformational Grammar
"peoples" the "emotional landscape"
with refutation.
You may hear its melancholy
long withdrawing roar
even on Dover beach watching
the undertow of all those trips
across to France.
Follow the reader and his writer,
those emblematic persons
along their mythic route
charting its uncertain curves and camber;
for to be true to any other you must—
and I shall never now—recover
a popular manœuvre known mostly as,
turn over
and go to sleep.

ON THE PERIPHERY

Ducks flee into the undergrowth
like eponymous heroes as we approach
the past, walking slowly on a path
beside a water-way or something.

These stories are committed to memory
and writing only when they have reached
a high degree of sophistication (we
have reached). Sanctioned and solacing
polythene buttercups strew our way
with images of "natural"
regeneration, inevitable.

Somewhere the table's set far from the traffic
jam, thus she spoke, turning, mov'd
the third heaven, that popular memory.
So many images now set revolving &
oh, that reminds me (poetry functions
as tribal mnemonic) who are we
having for dinner tomorrow.

THE AQUARIUM

Many pills, Matilda, does that make tonight?
But you *must* tell if you take the yellows.
The eyeball, listless under its tiny lid, moves
so slowly that downstairs in the cloakroom
were four rubber boots *all left feet* (this is a
Pedestrian Controlled Crossing but read as you
may you will find no mention of fish) covered even
ly with blood (groping in mud for a sound) whoever
however (and a collision is highly likely to occur)
controls the eyeball ignores this collision and takes
many yellows without telling any; hangs over books
brooding on mud. I, therefore, have nothing to add
to the scene transcribed above and the word that is
murder will fit very well. Over the boots but under
the eyeball are raincoats and hats and quotation
marks all wet through (or with name if you wish
to make plain the pills that we take for our)
into the garden it passes suffused now with pain
like an evening in spring the garland so fresh
and the roses so sweet she gave with intent to perceive.
Freckled by a glance the glass flickering advanc
es away into greenery untouched by the sun. Moreover
the grass also is green, so slowly the eyeball
did turn bloodshot in its emptying socket.

Note: see Roland Barthes: *S/Z, L'Empire des signes*
　　　　　Denis Roche: "Leçons sur la vacance poetique"
　　　　　　　in *Éros énergumène*
　　　　　Alain Robbe-Grillet: *La Jalousie*
　　　and Nathalie Sarraute: *Le Planetarium*

ON READING MR. MELVILLE'S *TALES*

When sunlight wounds me I think of thousands
it has killed on crowded beaches stripped like
knives whetted for sacrificial your hand is on my arm
your lips are on my cheek your eyes are on my eyes
whence water drips theories since Plato strolled
along those shores we have not seen such de
constructed presences of speech and sense so run
the traces through our history like scarlet woven in
a sailor's rope to say it is the King's (is any simile
more inappropriate) generally disseminated like take
O take your hands off me in the civilisation of the West
who ruled the evil and the good (some say that Claggart
is the devil) Shall I be cold and dead my love shall
I unweave the thread but we have superseded such banal
dichotomies as these or shall I join the rest in
holding off the meaning from the form lines present in inter
textual strands I should not like to hang despite Platon
Like Billy Budd my heart would stop; it has stopped;
the differment remains, remains and

Note: see Herman Melville: "Billy Budd, Sailor, an inside narrative"
Jacques Derrida: "L'Écriture et la différence" and
De la grammatologie
Julia Kristeva: *Semiotike: Recherches pour une sémanalyse*
and William Empson: "Missing Dates", *passim*

You never would have believed it could be so easy;
it played into one's hands, the unpremeditate paysage,
as Stevens said, crossing the fen, suddenly confronted
with such expanse of unpretentious waters as visit
our dreams. Elle resta, comme le dit Flaubert,
melancholique devant son rêve accompli.

Poetic diction performed for me two outstanding services:
in confirming that the subject I proposed treating
was a worthy one; and in feeding and clothing me
after I had, in a moment of abstraction, fallen
into Holme Fen Engine Ditch;

It partakes of the clay's history of human blood
and strife, like Devil's Dyke, our excursion to which
is hereby premeditated. Thus we are rescued from
the abstract ditch we dig with our fundamental
disagreement about the proper form for a picnic.

It is disturbing to find oneself on a level
with the river, smooth-flowing with pronouns
where we grub, like ducks, for whatever they eat,
in unexpected pools. A drastic diminution
of pronouns in the early weeks of marriage
(lack of third persons, not to mention more banal examples)
leads to this retracted meadow in which comparisons
must be deployed, the meadow she crosses now,
noting its blossoming synecdoches, on her way
to the library, carrying her *Heffers Cantab Students
Notebook, ref. 140, punched for filing.*

These daffodils are piston-rods which turn
faster and faster carrying (me). Insomnia
results from coffee and stimulating
company. Toilet rolls oscillate wildly
in all the cubicles as the train gathers
speed, etc. And so much for that image.
Exuberant pronouns flourish like baroque
cherubs in the spring air beckoning.
It would be possible to contact the
"actual world" if they flourished more
like the threatening anonymity of real
children, stumbled over in a street.
But this grace is denied (me).
Shoulder your skis or your umbrella and
glide with the pronouns over the bridge
past daffodils thumping like your
insomniac's heart, your shopping bag
is filled with the week's supply of
toilet rolls, which is a kind of integr-
ation between the image and reality.

And if Another knows I have a little nut-tree cultivated indoors
I know that in this climate nothing will it bear
despite much watering with sighs and tears.

I know little of horticulture but a silver anguish
supplemented by sundry domestic details not Christmas tinselled
and a golden fear of succumbing to the violet typing-ribbon,

Who only know that in return for the kiss you gave to me,
not here, O, Adeimantus, but in another world,
there is no more noise now I hand you the fruit of

More than a year struggling with the violet and the orange peel
which is so alien to my little nut-tree embedded
in the present context of its final version.

Note: the lines:
    "And if Another knows I know I know not
    Who only know that there is no more noise now"
    were omitted by Eliot from his final version, along with:
    "Not here, O, Adeimantus, but in another world".

    Pound was fond of using a violet typewriter ribbon.

PASTORAL

They are our creatures, clover, and they love us
Through the long summer meadows' diesel fumes.
Smooth as their scent and contours clear however
Less than enough to compensate for names.

Jagged are names and not our creatures
Either in kind or movement like the flowers.
Raised voices in a car or by a river
Remind us of the world that is not ours.

Silence in grass and solace in blank verdure
Summon the frightful glare of nouns and nerves.
The gentle foal linguistically wounded
Squeals like a car's brakes
Like our twisted words.

NOT PASTORAL ENOUGH

homage to William Empson

It is the sense, it is the sense, controls,
Landing every poem like a fish.
Unhuman forms must not assert their roles.

Glittering scales require the deadly tolls
Of net and knife. Scales fall to relish.
It is the sense, it is the sense, controls.

Yet languages are apt to miss on souls
If reason only guts them. Applying the wish,
Unhuman forms must not assert their roles,

Ignores the fact that poems have two poles
That must be opposite. Hard then to finish
It is the sense, it is the sense, controls,

Without a sense of lining up for doles
From other kitchens that give us the garnish:
Unhuman forms must not assert their roles.

And this (forgive me) is like carrying coals
To Sheffield. Irrelevance betrays a formal anguish.
It is the sense, it is the sense, controls,
"Unhuman forms must not assert their roles".

LE SIGNE (CYGNE)

Godard, the anthropological swan
floats on the Cam when day is done.
Levi-Strauss stands on a bridge and calls:
Birds love freedom; they build themselves homes;
They often engage in human relations.
Come Godard, come, here, Godard, here. The halls
of Clare and Trinity, John's and Queens'
echo the sound with scraping of chairs
and cramming of maws. A red-gowned don
floats by the swan. We must try to explain
to the posturing dancers that this is an image
of human existence; this is the barre-work
of verbal behaviour; this knife in the corpse
that they shove through a window to float
down the Cam when day is done
is Godard, the anthropological swan.

CONVERSATION ON A BENIN HEAD

You must come to terms with T.S. Eliot
If you are doing the twentieth-century.
At Girton my gloves and my heart under
My gloves. Words as they chanceably fall
From the mouth change colour whatever
The source, pages or brain or midway
Between window and chair. These colours,
Brown wood air grey ink black, we didn't
Create them. We don't believe they are there
Whatever they are or this is a dagger.
We *know* it's a dagger or nothing whatever:
A scream, a sentence, a phantom, a reading
Of Laing. Believe that my neck is supported
By circuits of communication, gold rings,
I know that and hundred in number, remember
Believe that my throat will collapse; flat
Nose and fat lips disintegrate quickly under
Your touch. Listen. I know it's a dagger.

Whatever it was I didn't do it.

A man must do something. If one
Thinks of other however the chances
Of seeming to cover a single event,
Not in the mind of the doer, the point
Of departure is hard to recover. It all
Goes to clothes and the moves
Of the wearer infinite in number
Between window and bed and he
Turned as he said it all goes to show
You have never been whether
Reluctant to swallow the trace of another
Or touch at your own. We'll collect
Them tomorrow. Such monuments over
The gathering quick of your pink
Little finger furrowing under the bone
Of my skull. Own this armour at least,
This stylistic skeleton caught in the last arabesque

but one.

THE EAR OF DIONYSIOS: ODE

for Linda Sparkes

Below the Greek amphitheatre
on the left of the Roman stadium
beyond the cord-makers grotto,
the monument thus named is found
to be one of the greatest engineering feats
of the ancient world. It was designed
for Dionysios, tyrant of Syracuse,
as a dungeon whence his prisoners' voices
would reach 1000 ft to his own less
permanent tympanum. If the tourist
will try the experiment he may hear
his own words echo throughout the
vast moist aperture. But Dionysios doesn't
listen any more. Je suis la victime et le bureau.

You are not like me; you are Giselle, Odette in this world of
similar asparagus (and no crummy puns on corps de ballet from
the audience; take your filthy words off her) or a waitress with
a Cockney accent. You are not like me; you are me in any of
these roles and your hair is not golden but brown if I want it to
be, and your body, mine in the bath.

All eras of decadence are as similar as asparagus; and I intend no
reference to Dowson's paidophilia, Swinburne's algolagnia or
Symons' cabaret dancers. These are monetary transactions
scented with white heliotrope.

Still white heliotrope
                 topic of still waters which run deep
when you are rowing
                 towing a growing sense of fear of
tropes in the boat.
             You can't return to the other shore
for it is before
             you rowed roamed and jumped
into the tangled isles.

                We are getting over-heated
and a second driver is risky
                        nevertheless refill the flask in Loch Ness
despite no road on the other shore.
                                And mother rows
over the scent in the bath.
                        It was a steep descent, helio
was nothing to it.
                Stagnant waters run deep and half and
you had better let me steer clear, dear
                                though I am ignorant of sailing and
the steering veers
                from shore to shore, I can give you
metaphor for metaphor
                        any day and get away along the
coastline of literary peaks
                        and threatening summits (Ben Ezra etc.—my crummy
                        puns)

        In places the mask slips the man shows clear
        with his bigotry hatred and fear;
        and in others his passionate tender heart?
        No, I fear art's a hard thing, my dear,
        there one sees just the greatness of art.

and plant their superfluous road-signs
                                long before for it is before
as aforesaid and "who
                are you anyway" said Mr. Ashbery before
who *lives* in New York
                (another 1400 ft peak)
if you are mother or the other
                        I can offer you no hope
therefore perhaps however you are:

        The dancer who is avatar with golden hair
        of everyone who has been lost. Should I not share
        her weary elbow on the barre. Rossetti

might have gestured thus. He named her this.
Yesterday she lost her bra. Some fetishists
are more banal than I who envy tears and sweat
for bleeding toes in satin shoes, enchainment
(Yeats') from mind to tree, but can't leap out of irony.
That they keep grace with such as she.

> an estimated 75% of Chinese restaurants
> in Paris are used as cover for spies. De spies.
> Replies to official questions were various,
> ranging from "we used to have some spies but
> they left; they didn't say where they were going;
> every restaurant has its ups and downs"
> to "sorry, no spies, but very good Peking duck".

> Je suis la victime et le bureau.

Memorial to the deportation. Whose? Jews. Yours. Ours. I consider this an insult to my staff about whom I am most particular; there are no spies here; anyway spies don't exist.
White blocks   black lines stone by   steel grille   by grille   line by line across the white and black block of the page.
There has been a new edition true to the new edition. (No God but confusion and Pound is its prophet; it floats on the sterling market. I smell a rat; I see it floating through the air; but I shall nip it in the bud. Ring-ring-a-roses, all fall down.) There has been a new edition of *L'Histoire de la folie* which costs too much; and in order to change your traveller's cheques you must return whence you came (a bench in the Luxembourg gardens) and know the place for the first time. Deconstruction
costs too much; le silence des siècles m'envahit; le tourbillonnement des siècles m'envahit. Il n'y a rien à te faire peur dès que tu monte ou que tu descend la tour de Notre Dame de Chartres. Montez-vous ou descendez-vous? She has a lightning-conductor on her back and from the tower you can see into the men's urinal (and know the place for the first time). I've never known what this fish was called in English, lieu: plaice? This is in memory of Max Jacob, paysan de Paris à paraître. Apparaîtra le pari et paresse d'être de la vie. La paresse des siècles m'envahit avec son révolver a cheveux blancs: animula vagula blandula   hospes comesque corporis   quae nunc abibis in loca   pallidula rigida nudula   nec ut soles dabis iocos. Facilis decensus Averno, this commemoration. But even Breton refrained from firing the revolutionary revolver. Revolving of revolution makes a priest always available; and you can teach its candles to burn bright. Facilis decensus Averno in deportation in

memory of Max Jacob. Rest in peace with the priest of revolution.
Quos nunc abibis in locos? Les billets ne sont plus valables au
Luxembourg.
If I think of a king at star-fall Ἀστὴρ πρὶν μὲν ἔλαμπες ἐνὶ ζωοῖσιν Ἑῷος

IN MEMORIAM EZRA POUND

obit first November
nineteen seventy two

Transpontine Ovid made his ovoid obsequies
unto the only emperor, the emperor of ice-cream.
In his elegies Teddy Bear is having picnics.
Can you find four ice-cream cornets hidden
in this elegiac picture? I pasture the pastel
colours of the heart, a part from and partial sense
of lethal elegies hidden in the provinces
of desolation and ice-cream, "the lost land
of Childhood", and the defeated past. Eyes
of a sleeper waked from fantasies (and this
is something more than fantasy) stance of a suicide
above the precipice of emptiness knowing that it must fill:
the fingers find the eyes and type. Take down the book.

Sometimes I think that this is the only thing, the
only stance, first slurp of ice-cream down the throat,
what Krishna meant as when he admonished Arjuna
on the field of battle. Pluck the petal
in the orchard where the factions act on emblematic
colours, red and white; leap with Nijinsky always
poised for entrance in *Le Spectre de la rose*. This
spectred isle, defying death with gesture. Awhile
to porpoise pause and smile and leap into the past.

He is not here he has outsoared the shadow
of our right. 'Tis life is dead not he. And
ghastly through the drivelling ghosts on the bald
street breaks the blank day of critical interpretation
staining the white radiance of eternity, every
little pimple had a tear in it, a fear of many
coloured glass, the noise of life strains the white
radiance of an elegy. How does the stress fall
on an autumn day. Remember remember the first
of November where history is here and nowhere:
the room in Poictiers where no shadow falls
on the pattern of timeless moments. Forget

the gate of white is the gate wherein our past
is laid. These books are radiant as time
against the shadow of our night where no
shadow falls. He is not dead.   Instead.

Give back my swing. O Ferris wheel.

STRIKE

for Bonnie, my first horse

I

Hail to thee, blithe horse, bird thou never wert!
And, breaking into a canter, I set off on the long road south
Which was to take me to so many strange places,
That room in Cambridge, that room in Cambridge, that room in Cambridge,
That room in Cambridge, this room in Cambridge,
The top of a castle in Provence and an aeroplane in mid-Atlantic.
Strange people, that lover, that lover, that lover, that lover.
Eyes that last I saw in lecture-rooms
Or in the Reading Room of The British Museum reading, writing,
Reeling, writhing, and typing all night (it's cheaper than getting drunk),
Doing tour en diagonale in ballet class (that's cheaper than getting drunk too).
But first I should describe my mount. His strange colour;
He was lilac with deep purple points (he was really a siamese cat).
His strange toss and whinny which turned my stomach
And nearly threw me out of the saddle. His eyes
His eyes his eyes his eyes his eyes
Eyes that last I saw in lecture rooms
His eyes were hazel brown and deceptively disingenuous.
I got to know those eyes very well.
Our journey through England was not made easier by the fact
That he would eat only strawberries and cream (at any season).
And he wanted a lot of that.
Nevertheless I got here and the first time I ever set foot in the place
I knew it was my home. The trouble was to convince the authorities.
Jobs were scarce and someone with a purple-point siamese to keep
In strawberries and cream has a certain standard of living.
When I sold my rings and stopped buying clothes I knew
It was the end. When I cut down on food it was clear
I was on some sort of quest.
There was an I-have-been-here-before kind of feeling about it.
That hateful cripple with the twisted grin. But
Dauntless the slughorn to my ear I set.

II

How many miles to Babylon?
Threescore and ten.
Can I get there by candlelight?
Yes. But back again?
From perfect leaf there need not be
Petals or even rosemary.
One thing then burnt rests on the tree:
The woodspurge has a cup of three,
One for you, and one for me,
And one for the one we cannot see.

III

What there is now to celebrate:
The only art where failure is renowned.
A local loss
Across and off the platform-ticket found
For the one journey we can tolerate:
To withered fantasy
From stale reality. Father, I cannot tell a lie;
I haven't got the time.
Mirth cannot move a soul in agony.
Stainless steel sintered and disowned;
Stars in the brittle distance just on loan.
The timetables of our anxiety glitter, grow
One in the alone. The cosmic ozones know
Our lease is running out.
Deserted now the house of fiction stands
Exams within and driving tests without,
Shading the purpose from the promised lands
No milk our honey.
And the train we catch can't take us yet
To the blind corner where he waits
Between the milk and honey gates:
The god we have not met.

THE LADY OF SHALOTT: ODE

The child in the snow has found her mouth,
And estate-agents must beware;
For if what we are seeking is not the truth
And we've only a lie to share,
The modern conveniences won't last out,
Bear tear flair dare,
And the old ones just don't care.

Back and forth she moves her arms;
Forth and back, her legs.
No one would care to say:
Her lips are red, her looks are free,
Her locks are yellow as gold,
Whether she's very young or old,
The nightmare life-in-death is she,
Who thicks men's blood with cold.

What of the future is in the past
Channels towards us now.
Present and future perfect past
Makes no tracks in the snow.
Turn the tap and water will come
For five seconds
And then the sand
Flows into our ever-open mouth.
What was it we understand?

She does not stand in the snow; she kneels:
A parody of prayer.
Lucretius said it long ago:
Why think the gods care?
When the telephone goes dead,
The fridge is broken, the light . . .

Why should we think of knowledge as light;
There is enough to see her.
And, having seen, the message is plain
To those who wish to know
(They are not many):
Run quickly back to darkness again;
We have seen the child in the snow.

Th'expense of spirit in a waste of shame
Is lust in action and, till action, lust
Until my last lost taper's end be spent
My sick taper does begin to wink
And, O, many-toned, immortal Aphrodite,
Lend me thy girdle.
You can spare it for an hour or so
Until Zeus has got back his erection.

Here where all trouble seems
Dead winds' and spent waves' riot
In doubtful dreams of dreams.
The moon is sinking, and the Pleiades,
Mid Night; and time runs on she said.
I lie alone. I am aweary, aweary,
I would that I were dead.
Be my partner and you'll never regret it.
Gods and poets ought to stick together;
They make a strong combination.
So just make him love me again,
You good old triple goddess of tight corners.
And leave me to deal with gloomy Dis.

Death never seems a particularly informative topic for poets
Though that doesn't stop them dilating at length upon it.
But then they would dilate on anything.
Love, on the other hand, however trite, is always interesting
At least to those in its clutches
And usually also to their readers.
For, even if the readers be not in its clutches
They think they would like to be
Because they think it is a pleasant experience.
I, however, know better.
And so do Sappho, Shakespeare, Swinburne, Tennyson and Eliot.
Not to mention the Greek dramatists:
Sophocles, Euripedes, Aeschylos, and Eliot.
We all know better.
Love is hellish.

Which is why Aphrodite is also Persephone,
Queen of love and death.
Love kills people and the police can't do anything to stop it.
Love will:
          ravage your beauty
          disrupt your career
          break up your friendships
          squander your energy
          spend every last drop of your self-possession
Even supposing you had such qualities to start with.
The god knows why we bother with it.
It is because it bothers with us.
It won't leave us alone for a minute.
For without us it wouldn't exist.
And that is the secret of all human preoccupation
(As others have said before me)
Love, death, time, beauty, the whole bag of tricks.
All our own work including, of course, the gods.
And we let them ride us like the fools we are.
Of all follies that is the penultimate:
To let our own inventions destroy us,
The ultimate folly, of course, is not to let them destroy us.
To pretend a stoic indifference, mask merely of stupidity.
To become ascetic, superior to the pure pleasures of the senses,
Arrogant and imbecile senecans, unconscious
Of what is going on even in their own bodies
Old whatsisname stuck up on his pillar,
A laughing stock, the ultimate in insensitivity.

The only thing, contrarily, to do with the problem of love—
As with all other problems—
Is to try to solve it.
You won't succeed but you won't make a fool of yourself, trying
Or, at least, not so much of a fool as those who refuse to try.
So here we go for another trip and hold onto your seat-belt, Persephone.

I loved you and you loved me
And then we made a mess.
We still loved each other but
We loved each other less.

I got a job, I wrote a book,
I turned again to play.
However I found out by then
That you had gone away.

My dignity dictated
A restrained farewell.
But I love you so much
Dignity can go to hell.

I went to hell with dignity,
For by then, we were three.
And whatever I feel about you,
I certainly hate she.

The god knows what will be the end
And he will never tell.
For I love you and you love me
Although we are in hell.

And what death has to do with it
Is always simply this:
If it isn't your arms I'm heading for
It's the arms of gloomy Dis.

SONNET

My love, if I write a song for you
To that extent you are gone
For, as everyone says, and I know it's true:
We are all always alone.

Never so separate trying to be two
And the busy old fool is right.
To try and finger myself from you
Distinguishes day from night.

If I say "I love you" we can't but laugh
Since irony knows what we'll say.
If I try to free myself by my craft
You vary as night from day.

So, accept the wish for the deed my dear.
Words were made to prevent us near.

FURTHER POEMS

A PLEA FOR EXCUSES

i.m. J.L. Austin

The clue discovered in a *performative*
verb promises completion to the poem;
it defines "the indirect free style"
by which narrators indicate these thoughts
are not of them, but of their creatures.

Free, that is, to impute our contingencies
to words, our creatures; indirect that
"is", since the object in parenthesis
is only "to be" experienced; and style?
well, this subject is to many a *nominal*

unhappiness, especially, articulate insincerity;
which let us avoid, creating for an object
the parenthetical excuse, and for a subject,
logical form:
    if . . . (the cat is on the mat)
  and if . . . (it is not the case that the cat is on the mat)
   then . . . (all possible worlds exist)

    if . . . (world is language)
  and if . . . (it is not the case that world is language)
   then . . . (all possible words are true)

Thus: all possible words exist and we are true
to none, unless the poem be performative
and promises that we exist (We promise
that it is.)
   There may be pleasure equally
in deploying the ambiguous richness
of unhappy words, and

      in   (placing
      the   delicate wrist
    against the   formica table-edge
      and   watching
      the   fingers
                   tremble.)

[1] The poet begins his story as he later ends it,
by placing Arthur's reign in historical perspective.
In one hand he holds a Christmas Tree
that is goodliest in green when groves are bare.
First the translation must preserve
the formulaic character of language:
disentangle invention from imitation.
An axe is not like a knife that carves a turkey.
If there be one so wilful my words to assay
let him leap lightly hither, lay hold of this weapon,
I quitclaim it forever; cranberry sauce is not like blood.
Our snowman is seen out of the window, in candlelight;
he is not a symbol of artifice.
Now lets make some plausible definitions, for example;
Beheading Game: the Dictionary Game, any reiterated
temptation to sever; Snowman: a symbol of artifice,
a kind of ceremonial boomerang; Getting Drunk
on Christmas Night: a wicked work, in words to expound.
We agreed to accept each other's pentangle;
this is called, The Exchange of Winnings.
For it is a figure formed of five points
to be token of truth, like laying the table.

THE TEMPTATION

I should have thought you: a squirrel,
hunted from a bird-table by images:
tokens of a non-verbal world, green
knights, rhyme schemes, Morgan le Fay:
signals with flashing lights for eyes
in the cut heads they hold towards you:
mouths full of adjectives and similes.
You would have claimed a kiss by your courtesy,
through some touch or trick of phrase
at some tale's end. You arranged:

the bedroom scene, the woodland scene,
the winter journey, the set table.
I should have held the mirror
for you to adjust your grammar.
At least accept this scrap of green silk,
as a protection from cranberry sauce
and other poetic analogies,
if you be Gawain, which I begin to doubt.

THE EXCHANGE OF WINNINGS

"Will you have some more white meat?"

I have a little hour-glass

I have a little hour-glass
Nothing will it give
But the trickling sound of
Water through a sieve.

All the bright neuroses
Sparkle as they go
Depression and obsession
Back and forth they flow.

Mingled at the bottom
One and one make two
Waiting the reverse, dear,
Quite like me and you.

I have a little nut-tree

I have a little nut-tree
Nothing will it bear
But a silver anguish
And a golden tear.

Now in return for the kiss
You gave to me
I hand you the fruit of
My little nut-tree.

IN MEMORIAM
for W.S. Gilbert

Such is my dream but what am I
An infant crying in the night
An infant crying for the light
And with no language but a cry

That everything should grow divine
If you and I could see and know
The world in one another so
If you were mine.

If you were mine to see and know,
No limit on this world of thine
Be caused by mine,
Except what you would choose to do.

You choose to do what you do show
You take the world away from mine
And make all thine
Hurting me by slow by slow.

Hurting me by slow by slow
When freedom, truth and skill of mine
Could make us great and strong in thine
I know,

The world could be our own I know
If you gave up the hurt of thine
And made life mine.
Apart from you the dark is mine.

Such is my dream; but what am I
An infant crying in the night
An infant crying for the light
And with no language but a cry

Such is my dream but what am I
An old acquaintance of the night,
But I could make all darkness light
If you would try.

CANZON
  for British Rail Services

Thou hast committed
fornication

Sols sui qui sai lo sobr'afan qe.m sotz

I know I am not the only to suffer the pains of love.
But this I also know: that each who loves thinks so.
For myself I can only say,
I doubt if any other
Has suffered more than myself
From this overloved desire.

It is always a wrong move
In the chess game of all we do;
It upsets the sparkling play
Whose light desire does smother;
It destroys all kind of breadth
And plunges a quagmire

My self is at one remove
Because it has gone to you
Who will not display
The sense of me another,
Being bound in yourself
By my forlorn desire.

Everything goes to show
That those are lucky who
Keep themselves away
From tangling with another
Cold and in themselves
Unlike my absurd desire.

I desire to love
You and be loved by you
Who cancel out my play
Being so much another
Being so much yourself
Away from my require.

You check my every move
By being what you will do
And not what I could say
To you, my love, an other,
Suffering more myself
By overlove and desire.

And yet I would not not love
If I could chose not to;
For I require to play
By hazarding myself
To you, my self, the other
Whom I always desire.

CODA

For
I am Arnaut who drinks the wind
And hunts the hare from the ox
And swims against the stream.

parody

immediacy

mythology of language

Re-writing of myths /old poetry

To those who kiss in fear that they shall never kiss again
To those that love with fear that they shall never love again
To such I dedicate this rhyme and what it may contain.
None of us will ever take the transiberian train
Which makes a very satisfactory refrain   *artifice*
Especially as I can repeat it over and over again
Which is the main use of the refrain.

I with no middle flight intend the truth to speak out plain
Of honour truth and love gone by that has come back again
The fact is one grows weary of the love that comes again.
I may not know much about gods but I know that
Eros is a strong purple god.   *Freud/Bloom*
And that there is a point where incest becomes
Tradition. I don't mean that literally;
I don't love my brother or he me.
We have been mutually avoiding each other
For years and will continue to do so.   *allusions*
Even I know about cross words—   *w/o*
Something. The word you want is Dante.   *meaning*
He said he loved Beatrice. Whatever he did
He didn't love Beatrice. At least the
Beatrice Portinari whom history gives.   *parody of*
He knew her and the point about all these   *the*
Florentines is that they all were   *waste-land*
Killing each other or dying of rapid
Consumption. Beatrice died; Rossetti painted her
Cutting Dante in the street. Botticelli
Painted the rest: Simonetta Vespucci
Died of a rapid consumption (age 23)
Guliano dei Medici murdered by the altar rail (age 19)
Guido Cavalcanti died in exile (age 35)
Dante dei Aligeri died in exile (age 90)
Lorenzo dei Medici who lives for ever   *doomed lovers*
Since he stayed there and commissioned
The paintings, and poems and statues

And if he also commissioned the deaths
I don't blame him. He didn't feel
Very magnificent when his brother
Was murdered in sanctuary.
Do you realise whoever did that
Would be excommunicated if, that is, if
He hadn't also murdered the papal legate,
His best friend.
I have lived long enough having seen one thing;
That term has an end.
It was getting dark on the platform of nowhere
When I who was anxious and sad came to you
Out of the rain. Out of the sound of the cold
Wind that blows time before and time after
Even Provence knows.
And as for this line I stole it from T.S. Eliot
And Ezra Pound and A.C. Swinburne. All very good
Poets to steal from since they are all three dead.
The love that is must always just contain
The glory of the love that was whatever be the pain.
We played at mates and mating and stopped up the drain.
Hear me. O Mister Poster I know
You have burnt me too brown you must boil me again
You simply have no notion how delightful it will
Be when they pick us up and throw us with the lobsters out to sea.
It is the lark, my love, and not the nightingale.
None of us will ever take the trans-siberian train.
She wanted to and was collecting people who did
I thought I did but now I know I don't.
It is the lark, my love, and not the nightingale.
In fact I've never heard either bird
But people say they sound very similar.
And what the devil were Romeo and Juliet
About wasting their last moments
Listening to birds. Hah.
I like kicking up larks or
Larking up kicks. So do most poets
Including J.H. Prynne, the memorable poet

105

Who is happy to say that the U.L.
Has got his middle name wrong.
He claims it stands for Hah
But there is a limit. I know it all.
Riddle me riddle randy ree
Round and round in the snotgreen sea
When they pick us up and throw us
With the Joyces out to sea.
Tell us tale of Troy's downfall
We all would have liked to have been there.
The infernal Odyssos. He it was whose bile
Stirred up by envy and revenge destroyed
The mother of womankind. And Swinburne
Got a kick out of pain but I don't
I just get kicked.
I wish I didn't keep sounding like Richard the Third
Except that if I don't I tend to sound
Like Richard the Second. And who wants that.
I suppose I must sound like Richard the First.
What did he do?
Nothing I take it
I get a kick out of larking up nightingales.
Prynne says that if I don't come back
Safe from Sicily by the thirtieth April
They will send a posse.
March is the cruellest station
Taking on bullying men
And were you really afraid they would rape you?
No. I thought there would be grave difficulties.
Not just that I was actively opposed
And so was every other man, woman and child
On that there train.
I was afraid they would kill me.
I may look stupid but I'm not
So simple as to think your name
Is Elizabeth Brown. Well. All right
My name is Veronica Forrest–Thomson.
Agammemnon was King of the Achaians at the time,

106

Priam, of the Trojans, Theseus, of the Athenians.
And like all Good Kings, they are dead.
In my day it was the done thing to side
With the Trojans for no better reason
Than that they lost. But me I back
Winners every time.
Mary Shelley may go to hell
As she thought she was going to anyway
And take Frankinsense with her.
I want her husband, alive and well.
Who, of course, also got killed.
Hardly surprising if he made a habit
Of reading Aiscylos while sailing.
He wasn't reading Aiscylos when he drowned.
Got cremated like a pagan king.
Not Agammemnon who, as I said, was king at the time
And lost, murderer of his daughter
Killed by his wife and (other) daughter.
Killed by his death killing his life.
Stabbed in the back in his bath.
I think of it every time I have a bath.
Though I have no sympathy at all
For that daughter and son.
I think it is unfair that Helen
Had everything, immortal beauty,
Lovers, cities destroyed and battles
Fought about her. And she just came home
And calmly went around being Menelaus' wife
While her twin sister, Clytemnestra
Was murdered by her son and daughter.
And the Athenians acquitted them.
They would do, a nation of sophists.
Always betraying their allies and torturing
Women and children and enslaving people.
They even killed Socrates, their one good man,
Then Plato tried to be a philosopher king.
And got enslaved for his pains.
I wish they had kept him enslaved.

[Handwritten annotations in right margin: "Freud?" bracketing "Mary Shelley... husband, alive and well."; "impatience ↑"; "debunking ↑"; "romantic images of the male romantic poetic"; "→ Percy Shelley" pointing to "He wasn't reading Aiscylos when he drowned."]

He escaped, of course, and wrote books
About how he would do it better
If he was in charge. All poets do that.
They are just as incompetent as the rest
If they try to organise things.
As witness my own efforts in that direction
Or those of my avatar, Agammemnon,
Who, as I say came home and was killed in his bath
Killing his wife and his daughter.
And if you don't know about this you ought to.
Read it in the *Iliad,* read it in the *Odyssey,*
Do not read it in Freud who is always wrong. ✓
Although even Freud didn't deserve a son like <u>Lacan.</u> *see Eagleton*
But first and last read me, the beloved
Who was killed in the general slaughter.
But rise again like John Donne   *feminising*
(read him too) I, Helen, I Iseult, I Guenevere,   *of classical*
I Clytemnestra and many more to come.   *women*
I did it, I myself, killing the King my father
Killing the King my mother, joining the King my brother.
It is the kick, my love, and not the nightingale
I like larking up kicks myself
But not kicking.
They that have power to hurt and do so
Should not be blamed by Shakespeare or anyone else
For hurting though such is the race of poets
That they will blame them anyway.
However it is a pretty productive process
Especially if one may be plumber as well as poet
And thus unstop the drain as well as writing
Poetic Artifice "Pain stopped play" and
Several other books and poems including
1974 and All That (seriously though)
I, Veronica did it, truth-finding, truth-seeking
Muck-raking, bringing victory.
It was a horse, of course, in which the warriors hid
Pretending to bring peace
And they wouldn't speak to me, crouching in the dark

Like a lot of fools, hearing the voice of the goddess
In an alien city, I speak your tongue in my own city:
Cambridge or Camelot and you won't listen to me
Advised, of course, by Odyssos, solicitor, betrayer.
And when they had killed all the men, raped all the women etc.
Agammemnon came home and, as I said, was stabbed by his wife
In his bath. Anyway it is the lark, my love,
And not the nightingale. I follow the sacred footsteps of
Hippolyta, the blest, the best
That has been said or spoken well in any tongue
Read John Donne—the memorable dun.
Don't read Matthew Arnold; he's a fool
I am not Prince Thomas Aquinas F.H. Eliot
I am not an attendant lord either.
I am the king who lives.   *— Freud/Wittgenstein/re-enterprets Bloom?*
Spring surprised us, running through the market square
And we stopped in Prynne's rooms in a shower of pain
And went on in sunlight into the University Library
And ate yogurt and talked for an hour.
You, You, grab the reins.
Drink as much as you can and love as much as you can
And work as much as you can
For you can't do anything when you are dead.

multiple
meanings

poem holds all

The motto of this poem heed
And do you it employ:
Waste not and want not while you're here
The possibles of joy.

alternatives to
spelling ~ meaning

re-invention
pop at Eliot
↳ so many meanings
waste not, want not

post-modern
version of a modernist poem
— allows reader a window into the poem
despite allusions
~ unlike Eliot

RICHARD II

The wiring appears to be five years old
and is in satisfactory condition.
The insulation resistance is zero.
This reading would be accounted for by the very damp condition of the building.
If you come up the stairs on the left side you will see
A band of dense cumulus massed on the banister.
Whatever you do, do not touch the clouds.
Forever again before after and always

In the light of the quiet night and the dark of the quiet noon
I awoke by a day side and I walked in time's room.
To the end of the long wall and the back of the straight floor
I stepped with my years' clutch and the dark of my days' doom.

For the sight of the deep sad and the swell of the short bright
Bid me flee waste of the time web and the long hand
On a life's weft and the grey warp in the year's cloak
For a long shade laps a short stand.

The terms left right front and rear are used
as if one is standing outside the building
facing the front elevation.
Specialists are carrying mirrors to the bedroom.
They are stacked beneath the window three foot deep.
Whatever you do, do not look in the mirror.
Again before forever after and always

The step to and the step back from the still glass in the long wall
Flung the glance wide from the old field and the brown scene.
And the glance broke at the pale horse on the glass turf
While the door swung where the window should have been.

With the ghosts gone and the wall flat as the clock's tick
With a blood stopped and a bone still I squeezed glue from my cold glove
And I turned back to my smashed self and the few looks pierced my own doll
From the back-lash of the time brick and the last wall of an old love.

In the joinery timbers there is new infestation
And a damp-proof course is urgently needed.
Say a few prayers to the copper wire.
Technicians are placing flowers in the guttering
They are welding the roof to a patch of sky
Whatever you do, do not climb on the roof.
Before forever after again and always.

limpid eyelid

S/Z

J'étais plongé dans une de ces
rêveries profondes
qui saissit tout le monde
même un homme frivole
au sein des fêtes les plus tumultueuses.

Au fêtes tumultueuses:
rêveries profondes.

I was sunk in one of those
profound daydreams
which grab everyone
even a trivial man
in the middle of the most violent parties.

At violent parties:
profound daydreams.

That is one of the rules Balzac uses
and Barthes notices.
There are many other rules,
but I don't want to mention them.
We can—some of us—sometimes
forget the whole problem.
I mean the only problem:
What is true.
I write no question mark
after that question.

There are a few answers, such as:
Literature matters.
What else is there.
What am I going to do with my life.
Write another book, I suppose.
What else is there.
I expect no answer.

Poems teach one that much:
to expect no answer.
But keep on asking questions;
that is important.
Just hope the house doesn't fall down
for I have no insurance.

Je suis plongée dans une de ces
rêveries profondes
qui saissit tout le monde
même une femme frivole
au sein des fêtes tumultueuses.

LEMON AND ROSEMARY

for Catherine Cullen

Nobody. I, myself.
Shooting live subjects in pictures sung with imagination and wrung with truth.
Dean knew it was blackmail.

Though my deserted frying pans lie around me
I do not want to make it cohere.
Hung up to dry for fishing lines on the side of grey wharf of Lethe.
Old, we love each other and know more.

Is this a chisel that I see before me.
If so I want to hack my name on the bedroom door.

A star shines on the hour of our meeting:
Lucifer, son of morning. And
Thanks for your lighter I have forgotten the matches.

O, why do I hate doctors so?
There was a time some years ago . . .
But do dial one O O O O

On the best battle fields
No dead bodies

APPENDIX I

Commentaries by the author written to accompany the publication of *Language–Games* and *On the Periphery* and the public reading of "Richard II"

1: NOTE

[Printed following the poems in *Language–Games* (Leeds, New Poets Award 2, School of English Press, University of Leeds, 1971).]

Most of these poems are obviously about the experience of being engaged in a certain activity, in a certain place, at a certain time: the activity, research in English Literature, the place, Cambridge, the time 1968-69. The attempt has been to deal with these elements as part of a "historical present" in which past language–forms, whether borrowed from poetry, letters, speech, or the dictionary, are made into a framework for a present act of articulation. This act looks for a form to express the poems' underlying theme: the impossibility of expressing some non-linguistic reality, or even of experiencing such a reality. Wittgenstein comes in here as I take his work to be the most stimulating exposition of the complexities involved in this view; but his ideas are also used to explore the second main pre-occupation of the poems, the relationship between "pure" intellectual activity, in fields such as philosophy and theoretical science, and their appearance in an "applied" context, as one element among others in one's attempt to make sense of concrete experience. It seems to me that this interaction is best seen as a juxtaposition of varying ways of using language for one is thus able completely to absorb the non–linguistic constituents of the experience into the art of language; questions of knowledge become questions of technique. This results in the setting up of a tension between the meaning of the ideas and statements in their original context and their appearance in the poem; they are in a sense different expressions, not because they refer to another area of experience—it is their own original area of reference that I have wished to make part of the subject-matter of poetry—but because they are used in a different way.

This kind of tension can be seen as a special case of the conflicts that arise from our constant attempt to integrate disparate levels of knowledge; it thus ties in with the exploration of the present sense of the past through its language–forms. At the vaguest level it could be subsumed under the grandiose heading of "Art versus Life"; for basically what we do with our words is what we do with our experience of living.

There is the opportunity to turn theoretical debate and abstract statement into a means of technical experiment in the actual medium of poetry, to explore new formal possibilities while extending the range of material dealt with. This involves an assimilation, not merely of the ideas but of the speech–forms of the relevant areas of discourse and even their methods of typographical layout. Certain poems here tentatively explore such possibilities. It will be seen that this leads to a new stress on the importance of "subject" in a poem; but because it is not the ideas merely but the actual linguistic forms that are to be the object of attention, the new kind of subject will be one that can be approached and even defined in terms of formal experimentation. The process is one of smashing and rebuilding the forms of thought. Thus one might be permitted to feel a certain affinity with those who see the role of the University as a subversion of accepted social reality. The means may be destructive however, but the end, or rather each particular end— for there are as many ends as there are poems—is not. The construction of poems becomes the record of a series of individual thresholds of the experience of being conscious; they form the definition, or affirmation, in time and in language, of human identity.

2: PREFACE

[In *On the Periphery* (Cambridge, Street Editions, 1976).]

The mysteries of this book are partially summed up in its title. After the head–on collision with non-poetic languages in my previous work I was faced by a stylistic situation on the periphery of traditional poetry. The sequence of pieces here represents—apart from their individual merit—a series of strategies for dealing with this difficulty. A difficulty which must confront any poet at this time who can take and make the art a new and serious opponent—perhaps even a successful alternative—to the awfulness of the modern world. I have argued elsewhere that this awfulness cannot be overcome with entire reference to the non-verbal world for the non-verbal world, like other deities, helps only those who help themselves. And what poetry gains from that world is gained through language, through the very languages that give us the world. For poetry, as always, has special access to aspects of language distinct from the aspect of communication. These simple, and very complex, mechanisms have been largely lost in English poetry since the 'twenties. So that my concern with French poetry and poetic theory and with ideas associated with "Structuralism" is a manœuvre of style, of verbal detail, as well as a manœuvre of theme and of social significance.

Hence the graph of this book begins in the extreme of aleatory poems, moves into simple lyricism confronting the claims of the external world with stylistic simplicity, reaches, in "The Dying Gladiator", an extreme of both technical and thematic complexity, and ends, in "The Lady of Shalott", by recapturing the right to speak directly through the traditional ranges of rhymed stanza.

The turning point comes in "Pastoral" where I realise in practice what I have long known in theory: that it is precisely those non-meaningful aspects of language—rhyme, rhythm and stanzaic metre are only the most obvious—which are poetry's strength and its defence. What had been tendentious obscurity of meaning becomes, therefore, a tendentious refusal of meaning, except the minimum needed to create verbal form at all, this coupled with a more assured and more traditional formal experimentation in the two Odes, the epitaph on Ezra Pound, the assertion of affinity with the past of English poetry, especially the neglected past of the late nineteenth–century, in "Strike".

Thus "The Lady of Shalott" is both the end of this quest for a lost imaginative freedom made actual in verbal detail and a beginning which, freed from sterile self–absorption, will move on to create new artifices of eternity. Thus also, the last poem "Sonnet" is the love poem I have tried throughout to write straight and have been held back from by these technical and sociological difficulties. For, as to theme, this book is the chart of three quests. The quest for a style already discussed, the quest for a subject other than the difficulty of writing, and the quest for another human being. Indeed such equation of love with knowledge and the idea of style as their reconciliation is as old as the art itself, for the other person is the personification of the other, the unknown, the external world and all one's craft is necessary to catch him. And, of course, being caught as a poetic fiction, as a real person he is gone.

And so one is left with the poems—what they do and what they suggest as possible. "For us there is only the trying / The rest is not our business".

3: RICHARD II

[Written to introduce Veronica Forrest–Thomson's commissioned poem 'Richard II' at the public reading in Southwark Cathedral of *Poems for Shakespeare* (part of the Shakespeare birthday celebrations) on 26 April 1975. A memoir of the circumstances of the reading, in her absence, of the poem and her chosen passage from Shakespeare, *Richard II*, V, v, 42-66, was published in A. Rudolf, ed., *Poems for Shakespeare*, 4 (London, Globe Playhouse Publications, 1976).]

This poem requires a little introduction which I hope will help you to understand what I am trying to do. I picked the play, *Richard II*, because it is one of my favourites and because it is one of Shakespeare's most striking uses of the image of the actor as hero. This image, of course, accompanies far-reaching meditation on the relationship between appearance and reality. The difference between appearance and reality and how poetry may bridge this difference by creating imaginative orders of words—for it is language that really mediates between the world of appearances and internal reality or the world of reality and internal appearances depending on one's philosophical position—has long fascinated me both in theory and practice. This problem and the problem of time are closely connected, for it is through time that appearance and reality interact, through time that poetry moves, and *Richard II* is therefore a play much concerned with time. These are the themes then about which or around which I wished to construct my poem but it would not do to sit down and write a versified meditation on time change appearance and reality. For this there are several reasons. First— though perhaps I should not let this out—I don't have very many or very new ideas about these topics at least just now. Second, ideas are not simply assimilated into poems direct but must make their way through the organisation of technical devices ranging from metaphor to metre. Third, and most important, I believe that at the present time poetry must progress by deliberately trying to defeat the expectations of its readers or hearers, especially the expectation that they will be able to extract meaning from a poem. A poem must work to transform the area of linguistic meaning into a technical device like rhythm or metre. Consequently the poem in question sets out to look as if it were a meditation on time, appearance and reality while in fact using these themes as points in its organisation as a metrical formal structure. It includes the normal expectations of the reader/listener but seeks to upset these in the interests of stressing the importance of non-meaningful levels of language in poetry. This is a more difficult undertaking from writing an ordinary poem as the balance of meaning and non-meaning must be very precariously set up. I think it must be attempted, however, if poetry is once again to take its place as an experimental exploration of the human mind working in language.

APPENDIX II

Uncollected early poems discovered since the publication of *Collected Poems and Translations*

THE ROOM

The air, so whitened   by the sun
that it's hard to tell where the light ends
and glass begins, is veined   by smoke
like   marble; life is a cigarette
puffed   by time; history an ashtray.

Once some surge of thought or feeling
welded these miscellaneous furnishings
into a mirror of the mind's   moment
reflected in their polished significance.

But now the timelessness of the inanimate
negates it;   the past, irrelevant
as death is to funeral ornaments,
has held nothing of them;
and the corpse coffined in an armchair
of memories is imperfectly embalmed by thought;
For objects slide   so quickly through the years
that already I'm beginning to decay.

Equator, [no. 2] ([Liverpool, 1966])

THE WHITE MAGICIAN

I

Oh Leonardo
do
you
know how
to screw
do you
no

how
the kite's tail
brushed
your mouth
at birth
and flew
to Milan
and back
again

playing Condottieri
tell us why
anything ever was begun
while learning how
to die
mechanics of anatomy
why try
to understand
a left hand.

If self is functionality,
Batman can do
better than you
so Leonardo
screw you
too.

II

A batwing's swing
stretches your brainspan,
spaceman,

draws our sinews'
twisting threads
to a spinning head.

Revolving blades
wind in the tensions
of light and shade.

Birds that soar
on your drawing board
never left ground,

for the work is done
when eye and object
became one.

But we can't tell you if any thing . . .
in our blueprint world,
a beholder's eye

blinds with the cataracts
behind that desperate flatness
of her smile.

III

Oh Leonardo
do
you
show how
to know
do you
no

how
Ludovico Sforza
thought so
of the lady
whose throat
you slit open with a stoat,
or Cesare Borgia
made war.
They were
too muddled for you.

Whose helicopter
dropped her
in the cup at the last supper,
the virgin on the rocks
of thought.

There are vineyards in Tuscany;
but oh Leonardo,
how can we about to die,
show you
why.

Continuum, no. 5 (Bailrigg, Lancs, [1967])

LITERARY HISTORIAN

I remember them saying,
these poems, their something
for someone at sometime
for me too, at one time.

That got in the way;
so I sent them away
back into history—
just temporarily.

They won't come back now.
I can't remember how
the words spoke, or what
they said,
except:
We are all dead.

Continuum, no. 5 (Bailrigg, Lancs, [1967])

APPENDIX III

Corrections to *Collected Poems and Translations* in respect of poems and commentaries not included in the present volume

PAGE	LINE	
all references		Identi–kit *not* Identi–Kit
133	5, 8	où *in the original French has twice been transformed as* or [ou], *possibly intentionally*
135	1	write here *not* write it here
143	4	that cry *not* the cry
146	1	*possibly* conventional *not* convention
178	3	persistent *not* persistant
193	5	It is true *possibly should be italic, the original French is, the F-T manuscript is not*
221	5	disguise *not* dsiguise
223	21	electrons *not* elctrons
233	3	*possibly* path at *not* pathat
233	11	*probably* its *not* it's
236	3	The ghost IS . . . the meat IS *not* The ghost *is* . . . the meat *is*
268	7	'Levels in Poetic Convention' . . . (1972) *not* (1971)
270	20	Denis *not* Denise
281		'Computor 97/100DV' was also printed in a version with very different lineation in *Continuum*, no. 5 (Bailrigg, Lancs, [1967])
282		'Catalogue' and 'Language Lesson for a Schizophrenic Age' were printed in *text*, no. 2 / no. 1 new series (Arnold, Notts., Autumn 1968)

POSTSCRIPT

Language, Experience and Identity:
An Introduction to the Work of Veronica Forrest–Thomson
by Alison Mark

Veronica Forrest–Thomson (1947-75) was a poet, literary theorist and academic whose work has been a central influence on the writing of subsequent linguistically investigative poets—poets who explore the inner and outer limits of language—in both Britain and the United States. In particular, since the publication in 1990 of the *Collected Poems and Translations,* her reputation has grown.[1] This selection of Forrest–Thomson's poems, notes and prefaces makes available to a wider readership the work of this remarkable poet, who was quick to respond in her poetic, as well as critical and theoretical writings, to intellectual and cultural theories which are now generally considered to be important. *Selected Poems* offers the opportunity to chart the development of Forrest–Thomson's poetic signature and approach to language, and also to explore the extraordinary referential richness of this body of work, which incorporates the range of traditional forms and the development of poetry in English through quotation, allusion and imitation.

Forrest–Thomson's importance, as both poet and theorist, lies in the radical innovation which characterises her work. Turning from her intitial engagement with British literary theory, especially that of William Empson, Forrest–Thomson's aesthetic was founded on her engagement with Wittgenstein's philosophy of language, and subsequently with structuralist and post-structuralist thought. Most significant in this respect are the work of Roland Barthes, of the Tel Quel group in Paris, particularly the semiotic theories of Julia Kristeva, and—largely through Kristeva—of Jacques Lacan. Forrest–Thomson was well in advance of her time in discovering these writers as important influences, and her articulation of critical theory in poetic language is a highly original contribution to poetics as well as to the development of a poetry whose power to move us emotionally as well as intellectually is often breathtaking.

There are three main themes in Forrest–Thomson's poems: identity, experience, and the representation of both in language. The innovative power and theoretical subtlety of her poetic work can be explored through a discussion of Forrest–Thomson's intricate handling of these interconnected themes, beginning with her use of that pre-eminent device of connection, the hyphen.

The title of the collection *Language–Games* (1971) is hyphenated, on the model of Wittgenstein's usage, and on the pattern of her chosen use of the hyphen in her own name. In her first collection, *Identi–kit*

(1967), published under the name Veronica Forrest, the hyphen in the title is used to call attention to the elements of the word, at once discrete and united. The device serves both to emphasise the theme of identity, and to indicate the possibility of discovering or creating through such poetic artifice a kit of tools for its investigation in language. A hyphen simultaneously draws attention to the split between two elements and attempts to bridge it, as described in her poem "The Hyphen";

> i hyphen (Gk. together, in one)
> a short dash or line used to connect
> two words together as a compound [. . .]
> But also: to divide
> for etymological or other purpose.
> (p 42)

Typically the line breaks—like the sign of the hyphen itself—underline Forrest–Thomson's theme here: "connect / two words", and "divide / for etymological or other purpose." These lines are constructed from the *Oxford English Dictionary* definition and intercut with other material to compare by juxtaposition the materiality of language with that of architecture and of history, for the poem is an occasional piece, written "*For the centenary of Girton College*".

A further split is manifested in the text of this poem by offset lines of typography:

> In search of an etymology
>   for compound lives . . .

These offer a physical mimesis of the internal split in the subject of which Forrest–Thomson was increasingly theoretically aware; an example of the self-conscious and self-reflexive use of language in her poetic work. The "lives" are compound rather than simple and unitary, and compound rather than singular: two lives (or language–games) joined together, for it is "the 'context in which we occur'" as much as the signification of "us" which dictates our meaning, according to Wittgenstein's theory of the language–game. His attempt to deal with the problems of communication involves not only the words which are spoken, written or thought, but the total context of human behaviour in which they are used. It is related to the later and more familiar post-structuralist concept of discourse.

"The Hyphen" ends with a "state- / ment of our need to hyphenate", that is to make connections, between things and between ourselves. But it also raises one of Forrest–Thomson's most pressing poetic concerns: the need to connect one element of language to another within the signifying system within the poem, as contained by its formal structure, rather than to refer immediately to the external world in search of meaning. This subject is discussed at length in Forrest–Thomson's posthumously published work of poetics, *Poetic Artifice: A Theory of Twentieth-Century Poetry*.[2] She recognised that a certain amount of "naturalisation", as she called the inevitable "attempt to reduce the strangeness of poetic language and poetic organisation by making it intelligible" (*PA* xi), is part of the legitimate work of criticism. But Forrest–Thomson deplored a premature rush to join words to world, to make a readily assimilable narrative of the poem, in which the power of the poem—greatest when held under the tension of formal containment—is lost, or diffused. She preferred that meaning be kept open, undecidable: to "make as many Naturalisations as possible and none certain." (*PA* 80)

The capacity of that which joins us together also to keep us apart—intrapersonally and interpersonally—that we see in "The Hyphen" appears again in Forrest–Thomson's work, notably in "Sonnet" (p 94), the final poem of her last, posthumous, collection, *On the Periphery* (1976). A traditional thematic of the sonnet form is the pain of sexual love, and we have grown used, since Freud, to expecting the torments of sexuality to be the source of most of the complexities of human experience and identity. Here the subtle line "Words were made to prevent us near" concludes this ironic, painful address to "the other", and the dislocated syntax preserves the sense of "us near" (us close), while using the word "prevent" (hinder) to impede and disrupt the conventional expectation of "bring" or "keep". Words were made to keep us apart, since they reinforce our separateness. Simultaneously her line preserves the seventeenth-century use of the word "prevent" as "to come before":[3] words come before our existence as subjects, alienated in language, and are at once our means of communication and creation of our world. At one and the same time they mark our capacity for union and for separation; embody communication and the blocks to understanding: we are divided by a common language.

In the Note following the poetry text of *Language–Games,* Forrest–Thomson describes the basis of her formal experiments in that text as an attempt to express "the poems' underlying theme: the impossibility of expressing some non–linguistic reality, or even of experiencing such a reality." (p 119) This is a theme she appropriated from Wittgenstein, and with which she plays in "Zettel":

> The concept of a living being
> has the same indeterminacy
> as that of a language.
> Love is not a feeling.
> Love is put to the test
> —the *grammatical* test.
> (p 32)

Here she cuts two statements from Wittgenstein's *Zettel,* and adds a final line.[4]   It is Forrest–Thomson's rearrangement in lineation, juxtaposition of two separate elements, and the setting in which they are embedded, which changes their status from that of the language-game of philosophy into the langauage-game of poetry, even though the words and their order are identical. The setting—the "context in which we occur", which she quotes in both "The Blue Book" (p 20) and "The Hyphen" (p 42)—and the typographical convention of poetic lineation are the two most important devices of poetic artifice that Forrest–Thomson employs here. They change our "conventional expectations, modes of attention, and interpretive strategies," (*PA* 22) as the quotations are moved from one discourse to another. Lexical units that are thus relocated carry with them the atmosphere and resonance of their source, but their meaning is given either an ironic twist or a powerful intensification: in the case of Forrest–Thomson's poems frequently both. The Wittgenstein quotations are: "The concept of a living being has the same indeterminacy as that of a language." (*Z* 59:326) And the memorable:

> Love is not a feeling. Love is put to the test, pain not. One does not say:"That was not true pain, or it would not have gone off so quickly". (*Z* 88:504)

Of course feeling is one possible philosophical ground of a non-linguistic reality. Forrest–Thomson's other citation of Wittgenstein on pain in "The Brown Book" (p 29), "trying to get between pain and its expression", also spotlights that missing link, non-linguistic reality, that can be detected behind Wittgenstein's interest in and handling of the subject of pain.

According to Wittgenstein a feeling cannot be put to the test of its "truth" in the way that love is, here. But why "the *grammatical* test", other than as a reference to the logical grammar Wittgenstein explored? Perhaps if language and identity ("the concept of a living being") are similarly indeterminate systems, then the same—"*grammatical*"—tests can be used to distinguish what is happening in experience as in language. The grammatical order in which one writes conveys the message of the sentence, and the construction of love can be tested by its ordering in time: does it last? Thus the argument: as love can be tested in language for significance by duration, while pain cannot, love is not a feeling, and so cannot be part of even that possible form of non-linguistic reality.

Forrest–Thomson's ommission of pain, the correlative that Wittgenstein uses to test love's status as a feeling, is intriguing in a poem that offers so powerfully what Suzanne Raitt calls the "extraordinary pleasure . . . of a licence to rest in a barely controlled distress",[5] where the capacity for emotional control is a correlative of the capacity for the exquisite control of the use of language. As so often in Forrest–Thomson's poetry, it is an instance of that which is withheld from full conscious expression being conspicuous by its absence, another "threshold" experience such as she describes in the conclusion of the Note to *Language–Games*, which also unites the themes of time and language in poetry:

> The construction of poems becomes the record of a series of individual thresholds of the experience of being conscious; they form the definition, or affirmation, in time and language, of human identity. (p 120)

Here the use of the word "thresholds" evokes that periphery of conscious awareness, implicitly also the periphery of the unconscious, to which the title of *On the Periphery* alludes. Forrest–Thomson explicitly connects the practice of poetry with an attempt to register, define, and by that definition to affirm, the experience of consciousness and identity. As time is the mediation of lived experience, so is language the connection between consciousness and identity; the mediating power of language is both their connection and the means by which, as structures, consciousness and identity are constituted:

> The basis of continuity between poetry and the rest of one's experience is the essentially verbal nature of that experience: the fact that it takes shape through language. What we can know of experience always lies within language. (*PA* 20)

The text of the Note to *Language–Games* relates closely the ideas of experience, identity, and an exploration of ways of using language, in order to turn the content of the poem into part of its form: "for one is thus able completely to absorb the non-linguistic constituents of the experience into the art of language; questions of knowledge become questions of technique." (p 119)

We can see this in "Antiquities" (p 39), where the technique creates a tremendous compression of sense:

> Glance is the copula
> that petrifies our several identities,
> syntactic superficies.

Glance petrifies; the gaze fixes and terrifies—and the suggestion is that it terrifies precisely because it fixes—that which it looks upon. We cannot forget the association of the Gaze with castration: looking and seeing present the most terrifying of gendered threats based on a phantasy of the meaning of sexual difference, yet are vitally constitutive of the subject. In these lines the *technique* of manipulating syntax, to which added attention is called by the use of the word "syntactic", absorbs and transforms this *knowledge*, while doubling the sense of the line. The glance—whose glance?—petrifies that upon which it looks. The child's first perception of identity at the Mirror Stage essentially devolves upon the gaze; Forrest–Thomson's conceit summons up a Gorgon whose power can frighten and freeze, whose gaze can be the "copula" that connects as it turns to stone—"petrifies"—our multiple and separate, our "several identities". And those identities are, like part of the art which informs these lines, "syntactic superficies"; clever arrangements of surfaces.

The two final words, suspended from the comma pause after "identities", highlighted by alliteration and by their position, indicates the tone of the entire verse of which these are the last three lines. This compression exemplifies Forrest–Thomson's attempt to "absorb the non-linguistic constituents of . . . experience into the art of language", where content becomes an aspect of form, and vice-versa. By "questions of knowledge become questions of technique", then, Forrest–Thomson suggests that by manipulating the formal elements of language the poet can give voice to that which cannot be spoken, and this is done through the effect of the poem on the reader, through their construction of its meaning. She equates the "non–meaningful aspects of language" of which "rhyme, rhythm and stanzaic metre are only the most obvious" (p 121) with the "non-linguistic constituents of . . . experience"—at least part of which must be feeling. The structure and devices form a net to catch that which cannot be expressed discursively, as in "Ducks & Rabbits" (p 30), Forrest–Thomson's poem about metaphor and the field of vision, where the image of a photograph is concealed in and revealed by the language play of the final verse. This perception, invited by the lines "Date and place / in the expression of a face", and confirmed by the "footnote" from Wittgenstein, "A child can talk to picture-men . . .", creates a sense of intolerable loss and longing at the conclusion of the poem.

In the exquisite "Canzon" (using a formal structure based on the Pertrarchan *canzone*), Forrest–Thomson again finds a way of speaking the unspeakable, describing the restless, self-defeating strategies of "forlorn desire":

> My self is at one remove
> Because it has gone to you
> Who will not display
> The sense of me another,
> Being bound in yourself
> By my forlorn desire.
> (p 102)

These lines offer an acute observation of the mechanism of projective identification. Here the subject's "self" is projected onto the other, which then fixes or confines the other as a phantasy object: "Being bound in yourself / By my forlorn desire." As such the other cannot be itself, which deprives the subject of the very thing it seeks, for then the other cannot reflect the "sense of me another"—the subject's own otherness for which in alienation it longs.

While the affective content of the earlier poems is predominantly pain, distress, grief, "a silver anguish / And a golden tear" , as the fruits of "a little nut tree" are described (p 90), in *On the Periphery* these are increasingly joined by rage and anger. "Drinks with a Mythologue" (p 69) marks the entry of violence—semantic and semiotic—into Forrest–Thomson's work. It is a sonnet of passion, of violence, rather than love: "violent" and "violence" appear explicitly, as well as "burst", "breakdown", "bursting" and "smash". The violence of dominance inherent in the effortless assumption of superiority in the "voice" of the "speaker" of the last three lines—in quotation marks to mark that speech—breaks through in the use of language and typography in this poem. In "S/Z" we can also see this violence rupture the surface of the poem in the shock of her translation of Balzac's "fêtes tumultueuses" as "violent parties" (p 112). It is a verbal violence, at the level of the signifier, not simply a semantic violence, that is imaged in the typographic splitting of "Drinks with a Mythologue".

This splitting, with intermittent suturings (verbal hyphens) as in "Drinks with a Mythologue", begun in *Language-Games*, recurs in several of the poems of *On the Periphery*, poems of a period in which Forrest–Thomson was explicitly conscious of her position at the borderline between tradition and "avant-garde" resistance in poetry in English, as she demonstrates in the preface:

> The mysteries of this book are partially summed up in its title. After the head-on collision with non-poetic languages in my previous work I was faced by a stylistic situation on the periphery of traditional poetry. The sequence of pieces here represents— apart from their individual merit—a series of strategies for dealing with this difficulty. (p 121)

One of these strategies is the play of allusion and quotation from poetic rather than non–poetic languages, increasingly a feature of her work, and allied with this the development of what foreshadows a postmodern use of parody, which can choose between, and even alternate between, humorous irony and serious tribute, as it negotiates the double part of conservation and transgression, tradition and resistance. This figures in her employment of traditional forms, like the villanelle and sonnet, and in poems like "The Lady of Shalott: Ode" (p 90), and "The Garden of Prosperine" (pp 91-93). The technique meets and marries in many of the poems in *On the Periphery*—not least in "Drinks with a Mythologue"—with her interest in French poetry and theory.

With the poem "Richard II" (pp 110-111), in a characteristic resistance to the bifurcation of literature and theory, she again declares her position. This poem deals with precisely the issue of the condition of the house of poetry, "on the periphery" between the conservation of poetic tradition and the possibilities of renovation offered by new techniques. Recapitulations of earlier poetic techniques are cut with a material depiction of an exploratory tour of a decaying house. "Richard II" ends with an extraordinary performance on the very roof of that house, which attests both to Forrest–Thomson's beliefs about the future of poetry, and the potential of what she called "non–meaningful levels of language" (p 124; *PA* xiv) in the detached, floating, unmotivated, unpunctuated final line:

> In the joinery timbers there is new infestation
> And a damp-proof course is urgently needed.
> Say a few prayers to the copper wire.
> Technicians are placing flowers in the guttering
> They are welding the roof to a patch of sky
> Whatever you do, do not climb on the roof.
> Before forever after again and always.
>
> limpid eyelid
> (p 111)

The materiality of language and poetry is compared to the materiality of experience, but in a material world in which a surreal welding of the roof to the sky can be envisaged, in which forever, before, after and again can shift the sequence in which they appear, as they do in the mutating refrain. The performativity of Forrest–Thomson's poetry is in evidence in this meditation on Richard II's final soliloquy, in which Richard seeks to "compare / This prison, where I live, unto the world", and Forrest–Thomson to "compare" the prison-house of language with the external world.

In her Introduction to the poem she says:

> I believe that at the present time poetry must progress by
> deliberately trying to defeat the expectations of its reader or
> hearers, especially the expectation that they will be able to extract
> meaning from a poem. (p 123)

In *Poetic Artifice* she offers a further gloss on this: "If poetry is to justify
itself . . . it must assimilate the already-known and subject it to a
reworking which suspends and questions its categories, provides
alternative orderings." (*PA* 53) And this it does against the pressure of
the reader's desire to interpret words back into world, to "make sense"
of the poem, immediately to naturalise it into a readily intelligible
narrative.

In "Cordelia: or, 'A poem should not mean, but be'" (pp 104-109)
first published in the Omens Poetry Pamphlet of that name (1974),
parody becomes an increasingly important technique, developing from
Forrest–Thomson's use of other language–games in that of poetry, but
there are other poems which prepare the ground for the negotiations
with parody and gender that appear there. Throughout her poetry she
uses parody as a technique, as part of her "kit for transforming the non-
poetic into the poem" (*PA* 129), rather than just to achieve a satiric or
burlesque effect; but it is in her recuperations of Romantic and
Victorian poetry in the poems of the collection *On the Periphery* that
the connection between parody and gender is made.

Gender begins to be refigured in Forrest–Thomson's work of this
period by her employment of the figure of Persephone, in "The Lady of
Shalott", and of course in "The Garden of Prosperine". Both of these
take their titles from well–known poems by nineteenth–century male
poets, Tennyson and Swinburne. Male poets have traditionally
apostrophized female figures, and exploited them as both structural and
thematic devices. They have used female fictional personae to hold their
poems together, either entirely within the poem as its subject like
Tennyson's "Lady of Shalott", or by implication as the addressees or
objects of poems, like so many of Donne's and Empson's clearly female
"you"s. The fictional females, who are related to the female "Muse"
beloved of male poets, are frequently dangerous and/or occult—at least
to the male subjects of the poems in which they appear. These mutating

figures are "denizens of Pastoral" (*PA* 118) in the sense that they are instruments of artifice and function on the structural as well as thematic levels of the poem. Forrest–Thomson's own capacity for alternation between resistance to tradition—an innovative disruption of expectation—and the adoption of formal techniques of rhyme and metre inherited from that tradition, as well as its themes and thematic personae, is productive of powerful poetry. She finds the middle area— on the periphery of both tradition and innovation—through an articulation of parody.

In "Cordelia" the beginning of a move towards establishing the inheritance of the female line set up by her earlier use of Persephone is developed in her reworkings of patriarchal myth:

> I, Helen, I Iseult, I Guenevere,
> I Clytemnestra and many more to come.
> I did it, I myself, killing the King my father
> Killing the King my mother, joining the King my brother.
> (p 108)

A description of descent, of identification, which does not ignore the lethal implications of the process of inheritance, of succession, of the Oedipal situation. Her assertion and identification of the poetic "I" here is neither restricted to powerful mythical figures of women, nor to a subordinate position, whatever the inheritance from the predominantly male tradition. She draws attention to the fact that persons, even historical persons or the living, once set in a poem are not "themselves" but fictional constructions: Dante's Beatrice is not "the / Beatrice Portinari whom history gives" (p 104). Towards the conclusion of "Cordelia" Forrest–Thomson goes on to assert the status of the "I" of this poem, who is clearly a poet though not necessarily to be identified with the poet who is writing (even if her name has already been given as part of the substance of the poem):

> I am not Prince Thomas Aquinas F.H. Eliot
> I am not an attendant lord either.
> I am the king who lives.
> (p 109)

Cordelia never actually appears in the body of the poem, perhaps inevitably, since Cordelia was remarkable for silence—love and silence. The very use of Cordelia's name thus evokes that silencing of the female poetic voice occasioned by the significant exclusion of woman poets from the literary canon, and in particular from the discourse of the epic.

As well as affirming the continuity of poetic identity, through the medium of poetry—in this case, of parodic epic, at once serious and humorous—Forrest–Thomson also interrogates identity, which might be either false or assumed, before discussing her own, under the guise of answering an implied question from an implied interlocutor:

> I may look stupid but I'm not
> So simple as to think your name
> Is Elizabeth Brown. Well. All right
> My name is Veronica Forrest–Thomson.
> (p 106)

And thereby turns herself into a poetic persona or "I", simultaneously factual and fictional. As she remarks in *Poetic Artifice:* "Of course I have been maintaining all along that the personages and decor in poems are convenient fictions, and that so are the poet and reader" (*PA* 69), figures of speech rather than figures of flesh.

Her earlier practices of embedded quotation and allusion develop in "Cordelia" into a sustained and sophisticated use of parodic technique to maintain connections simultaneously between different discourses, different languages, different aspects of the history of poetry and poetic language, and to disrupt expectation, effect discontinuity and transgress the authority on which they initially draw. Forrest–Thomson evolved this technique in her search for the middle ground in which new meanings—new "imaginative possibilities in the future" as she says in the preface to *Cordelia*—can develop, a middle ground on the periphery of both tradition and innovation where what was previously silenced can begin to speak.

The preface to *On the Periphery*, her last collection of poems, concludes with the words: "And so one is left with the poems—what they do and what they suggest as possible. 'For us there is only the trying / The rest is not our business'" (p 122).[6] There remains to us a substantial body of poetic work that in accomplishment far exceeds and frequently diverges from the proscriptions and prescriptions of

Forrest–Thomson's own poetics, criticism and commentaries. "What they do" is indeed to offer a unique "record of a series of individual thresholds of the experience of being conscious" (p 118), which illuminates the question of the nature of the relationship between experience, identity and language: what it is to be a subject, located in time and language. "What they suggest as possible" is a continuation of her courageous exploration in poetry of how "what we do with our words is what we do with our experience of living." (p 120)

> Poems teach one that much:
> to expect no answer.
> But keep on asking questions;
> that is important.
> ("S/Z", p 113)

NOTES

1.   Veronica Forrest–Thomson, *Collected Poems and Translations*, ed. Anthony Barnett, (London, Lewes, Berkeley: Allardyce, Barnett, 1990). In this Afterword I have drawn on material from: Alison Mark, *Veronica Forrest–Thomson and Language Poetry* (Plymouth: Northcote House/British Council, forthcoming); "Reading Between the Lines: Identity and the Early Poems of Veronica Forrest–Thomson", in *Kicking Daffodils: Essays on Twentieth-Century Women's Poetry*, ed. Vicki Bertram (Edinburgh: Edinburgh University Press, 1997), pp 210-26; "Hysteria and Poetic Language: A Reading of the Work of Veronica Forrest–Thomson", *Women: A Cultural Review* 5:3 (1994), pp 264-77; "Veronica Forrest–Thomson: Towards a Linguistically Investigative Poetics", *Poetics Today* (forthcoming) "Poetic Relations & Related Poetics: Veronica Forrest–Thomson & Charles Bernstein", in *Assembling Alternatives*, ed. Romana Huk (Hanover, NH: Wesleyan University Press, forthcoming).

2.   Veronica Forrest–Thomson, *Poetic Artifice: A Theory of Twentieth-Century Poetry* (Manchester: Manchester University Press, 1978); hereafter *PA*.

3.   I am indebted to Helen Carr for reminding me of this usage.

4.   Ludwig Wittgenstein, *Zettel*, ed. G.E.M. Anscombe and G.H. von Wright, trans. G.E.M. Anscombe (Oxford: Blackwell, 1990); hereafter *Z* .

5.   Suzanne Raitt, "Veronica Forrest–Thomson *Collected Poems and Translations*", in *Women: A Cultural Review,* 1:3 (1990), pp 304-8 (305).

6.   "For us, there is only the trying. The rest is not our business." This is the form in which it appears in T.S. Eliot's "East Coker" from *Four Quartets*, in *Collected Poems 1909-1962* (London: Faber and Faber, 1963), p 203. It comes at the end of a passage which explores the difficulty of writing, and Forrest–Thomson quotes it after describing her own "quest for a subject other than the difficulty of writing" (p 122).

INDEX OF TITLES